In-depth Small Group Bible Studies

STUDY GUIDE

10 Commandments

10 COMMANDMENTS

our guide for thankful living

Joel Kok

Grand Rapids, Michigan

Unless otherwise noted, Scripture quotations in this publication are from the HOLY BIBLE, NEW INTERNATIONAL VERSION, © 1973, 1978, 1984, International Bible Society. Used by permission of Zondervan Bible Publishers.

Cover photo: Corbis

Word Alive: In-depth Small Group Bible Studies

We welcome your comments. Call us at 1-800-333-8300 or e-mail us at editors@faithaliveresources.org.

www.FaithAliveResources.org

ISBN 978-1-56212-850-0

10 9 8 7 6 5 4 3

Contents

Introduction

Now that Christ has come and fulfilled God's law, do we still need the Ten Commandments? Of course!

As Joel Kok, the author of this study, explains on the basis of Scripture, Christ came to fulfill God's law so that we could follow his example and live by the law too, which we weren't able to do on our own. As believers in Christ empowered by his Spirit, we are called to follow the Ten Commandments as a summary of God's law, the *torah,* every day.

But as new creatures in Christ, we are not called to dwell on the negative expressions of this Old Testament law. Sure, we must admit and confess the guilt this law convicts us of, for we are still sinners while we're gradually growing perfect in Christ (2 Cor. 3:18; 1 John 1:8-9). But in the hope we now have in Christ, our Lord calls us to search out and live by positive expressions of God's commands so that we can carry on the mission Jesus began for this world already two thousand years ago: showing and telling others everywhere about his good news of salvation.

How long will this mission last? We don't know. But we do know where it will lead and who leads it.

That has to be enough for us now while we travel the way of life our Lord Jesus lays out for us each day. And we know he'll be "with [us] always"—through tortuous, tough passages as well as in pleasant places—as we go God's way, following Jesus and teaching others about the Christ-fulfilled law as our guide for thankful living (Matt. 20:19-20).

May God the Father, Christ the Son, and the Holy Spirit fill you with joy as you study God's law and search out ways to apply it thankfully each day.

—Paul Faber, for Faith Alive Christian Resources

Joel Kok, author of this study guide and the accompanying leader's guide, is a Christian Reformed pastor in Broomall, Pennsylvania. He has also served as a pastor in Ames, Iowa, and as an adjunct professor of Bible at Eastern University, St. David, Pennsylvania, and at Eastern Baptist Theological Seminary, Wynnewood, Pennsylvania.

How can we choose life?

1

DEUTERONOMY 5:7; 6:4-25

Beginning with God

In a Nutshell

The first commandment prohibits having other gods besides the Lord, the one true God (Deut. 5:7). Expressed positively, the first commandment calls us to love the Lord our God with all our heart and soul and strength (6:5). When we love the Lord first of all, we inevitably teach that love in all our relationships. For this reason, obedience to the great commandments (Matt. 22:34-40) leads to fulfilling our Lord's great commission (28:16-20). For both ourselves and our neighbors, to choose obedience is to choose life (30:15-20).

Deuteronomy 5:7

"You shall have no other gods before me."

Deuteronomy 6:4-25

4Hear, O Israel: The LORD our God, the LORD is one. 5Love the LORD your God with all your heart and with all your soul and with all your strength. 6These commandments that I give you today are to be upon your hearts. 7Impress them on your children. Talk about them when you sit at home and when you walk along the road, when you lie down and when you get up. 8Tie them as symbols on your hands and bind them on your foreheads. 9Write them on the doorframes of your houses and on your gates.

10When the LORD your God brings you into the land he swore to your fathers, to Abraham, Isaac and Jacob, to give you—a land with large, flourishing cities you did not build, 11houses filled with all kinds of good things you did not provide, wells you did not dig, and vineyards and olive groves you did not plant—then when you eat and are satisfied, 12be careful that you do not forget the LORD, who brought you out of Egypt, out of the land of slavery.

13Fear the LORD your God, serve him only and take your oaths in his name. 14Do not follow other gods, the gods of the peoples around you; 15for the LORD your God, who is among you, is a jealous God and his anger will burn against you, and he will destroy you from the face of the land. 16Do not test the LORD your God as you did at Massah. 17Be sure to keep the commands of the LORD your God and the stipulations and decrees he has given you. 18Do what is right and good in the Lord's sight, so that it may go well with you and you may go in and take over the good land that the LORD promised on oath to your forefathers, 19thrusting out all your enemies before you, as the LORD said.

20In the future, when your son asks you,
"What is the meaning of the stipulations,
decrees and laws the LORD our God has
commanded you?" 21tell him: "We were
slaves of Pharaoh in Egypt, but the LORD
brought us out of Egypt with a mighty
hand. 22Before our eyes the LORD sent
miraculous signs and wonders—great and
terrible—upon Egypt and Pharaoh and his
whole household. 23But he brought us out
from there to bring us in and give us the
land that he promised on oath to our forefathers. 24The LORD commanded us to obey
all these decrees and to fear the LORD our
God, so that we might always prosper and
be kept alive, as is the case today. 25And if
we are careful to obey all this law before the
LORD our God, as he has commanded us,
that will be our righteousness."

Additional reading: Deuteronomy 30:15-20

Urgent Questions

In high school Raheem Bath scored 1440 on his SAT and was accepted at Duke University. In college he majored in electrical engineering and economics. Though usually a disciplined student, Raheem got drunk on November 15, 1999, passed out in his bed, and vomited. While asleep, he inhaled some of his own vomit. This led to an infection that developed into pneumonia. Less than two weeks later, on November 27, this promising young man died.

Since that time, Raheem's mother, Catherine Bath, has carried out a mission against both the alcohol industry and the moral sickness in North American society that she believes contributed to her son's death. Her inspiration for this mission comes, she says, from God. But Mrs. Bath does not follow God as interpreted in the Christian tradition. In reaction to her son's tragic death, she has rejected both conventional American materialism and the contrary alternative of the drug culture, and she and her husband, Tom, have embraced Islam. The story of the Bath family raises several urgent questions:

- *How shall we live?*
- *How can we persuade young people to reject ways of self-destruction and to choose life?*
- *How can we escape the slavery of materialism?*
- *How can we persuade our neighbors to follow Jesus Christ?*

Start with Your Own Heart

To questions like these Deuteronomy 6 provides a divinely revealed response. The LORD reveals himself as the one true God (Deut. 6:4) and then issues this first and greatest commandment: "Love the LORD your God with all your heart and with all your soul and with all your strength" (6:5; see Matt. 22:37). Obedience to this command begins by allowing God's words to sink into our own hearts (Deut. 6:6). Once we have chosen obedience, life, and God by listening wholeheartedly to God's words, we can proceed to teach others. This teaching mission begins in our own households with the people who are closest to us, and from there it expands. "Impress [God's words] on your children. Talk about them when you sit at home and when you walk along the road, when you lie down and when you get up" (6:7). In other words, obey and teach God's words at all times and in everything you do.

Note the logic of the first commandment. It comes first because God matters more than anything else. Obedience to it begins with our own heartfelt listening to God. With these priorities in place, we will inevitably participate in God's mission not only to each new generation but to "all nations" (Matt. 28:19). We will make disciples as we learn discipline in the ways of God. We will teach love for God by loving God ourselves. We will promote obedience and life by choosing, in God's strength, to live obediently. In a word, we will fulfill the great commission by obeying the great commandments. As we come to know "the only true God, and Jesus Christ, whom [God has] sent" (John 17:3), we will receive power to pass that knowledge along to our children and to "all who are far off—for all whom the Lord our God will call" (Acts 2:39).

No Other Gods

Deuteronomy 6 gives positive expression to the first commandment. We should note, however, that in the Decalogue (Ten Commandments) itself (see Ex. 20; Deut. 5) the first commandment comes in the form a prohibition: "You shall have no other gods before me" (Deut. 5:7). So in order to say yes to the one true God, we need to say no to all other gods.

In a book titled *Do We Still Need the Ten Commandments?* a Christian teacher named John H. Timmerman asserts, "The greatest threat to true religion today may be the cult of the individual." He notes that when we serve anything other than the one true God, "what we really choose are our own desires and ambitions—ourselves in other words." Timmerman concludes, "The basic choice in our lives, then, is this: the worship of God or the idolatry of self."

If, like Timmerman, we observe further that "the cult of the individual" often reveals itself in whipsaw fashion by taking the form of reactive conformism (like ex-hippies who become legalists or materialists), we can agree that the basic choice we all face is *Will we worship God or ourselves?*

In the Beginning

When we state the choice abstractly, we know we must choose God. But how can we express that in flesh-and-blood terms in our day-to-day living?

We can go back to Deuteronomy 6 and note that loving God takes the form of letting God's words sink into our hearts (6:6). We can worship God rather than ourselves by making listening to God the main thing we do each day. In other words, we can follow the way of Psalm 1, which teaches us to say no to self-centered ways that lead to destruction and yes to the God-centered way that leads to life. In this way we can meditate on God's words "day and night" (Ps. 1:2).

This is the way Jesus followed during his entire ministry leading up to the cross. Jesus meditated on and depended on God's words in the wilderness (Luke 4:1-13), and he habitually carved out time at daybreak to listen to his heavenly Father (see 4:42; 5:16). Having impressed God's words on his heart, Jesus was prepared to say no to Satan and to self and yes to God and to love. Led by the Spirit and instructed by the Father's words, Jesus fulfilled Deuteronomy 6:13, which he quotes as follows: "Worship the Lord your God and serve him only" (Luke 4:8). By beginning with the heavenly Father, Jesus could begin carrying out God's mission to the ends of the earth.

Personal Pentecost

Many believers and congregations want to become more evangelistic. Sometimes they see Christian tradition as opposing that desire. But when we understand both mission and tradition biblically, we see that they go together. Following the pattern of Deuteronomy 6 as fulfilled in Jesus Christ, we can become equipped as evangelists by loving God in the form of listening to God's words and living by them. We can carry out God's mission by teaching the Scriptures to those who are closest to us. And from there God's Spirit can lead us to be Jesus' "witnesses . . . to the ends of the earth" (Acts 1:8).

Additional Notes

Deut. 6:4—In the Jewish tradition, this passage is known as the Shema, from the Hebrew word for "hear." Observant Jews recite the Shema twice each day, morning and evening ("when you lie down and when you get up"—6:7), as a confession of faith and as a declaration of loyalty to and love for God. Disciplined Christians can adapt this practice for their own devotional exercises.

The word "LORD," when printed in Scripture with large and small capital letters, is a rendition of Israel's covenantal name for God. This name is also referred to as the Tetragrammaton, from the four Hebrew consonants that we transliterate into English as *YHWH* or *YWVH*. Later Jewish piety forbade the pronunciation of this name for God, so no one knows exactly how it was pronounced. In some older Bible translations this name for God is rendered as "Jehovah." In some modern translations it is rendered as "Yahweh." In whatever form we encounter this name for God, we do well to associate it with the biblical idea of God's covenant faithfulness to Israel. (See Ex. 3:13-15 for an important passage in which God reveals himself to Moses as "the LORD.")

The NIV and other Bible versions provide textual notes indicating that the grammar of Deut. 6:4 allows for several possible translations. Translations that say, "the LORD is one," bring out the biblical teaching of monotheism, that there is only one God. Translations that say, "the LORD alone," bring out the exclusive character of the LORD's covenant relationship with Israel.

6:5—The biblical, covenantal understanding of love connotes not only or even primarily an emotional state but rather a loyalty expressed in obedience, evident in Jesus' statement "If you love me, you will obey what I command" (John 14:15).

In the Old Testament the heart is the seat not only or even primarily of the emotions. It is first of all the seat of thinking and willing, and it stands for a whole self dedicated either to God or to something that is not God (see Prov. 4:23). Note that the New Testament version of this command depicts Jesus as saying, "Love the Lord your God with all your heart and with all your soul and with all your mind" (Matt. 22:37). In this way Jesus echoes the holistic understanding of personhood and the intellectual character of love taught in this passage of Deuteronomy.

6:6—"These commandments . . . are to be upon your hearts." More literally, this statement is telling God's people, "Take these words to heart"—"words" being a reference to the Ten Commandments. In 4:13 we find the same Hebrew word used in the phrase translated as "the Ten Commandments," which can be more literally translated as "the Ten Words" (see also 10:4). As noted in the comments above, the Ten

Commandments are also sometimes referred to as the Decalogue (from the Greek *dekalogos*), which also means "ten words."

6:20-25—This passage illustrates the role of the family in transmitting biblical faith. For another example of mission in the form of familial instruction, see Exodus 12-13. Through repeated familial instruction, each generation of Israelites learned to appropriate God's saving acts in history by saying, "I do this because of what the LORD did for me when I came out of Egypt" (Ex. 13:8). The apostle Paul reflects this same biblical way of thinking when he says, "We were therefore buried with [Christ] through baptism into death in order that, just as Christ was raised from the dead through the glory of the Father, we too may live a new life" (Rom. 6:4).

GENERAL DISCUSSION

1. In what ways to do we still struggle with serving "other gods" today?

2. Read Deuteronomy 6:4-9. (During your session, try reading it in unison.) Does this passage describe how you live? Do you find it appealing? Explain.

3. Do you agree with this statement by Eugene Peterson: "The family is a most useful, maybe the most useful, arena in which to learn the faith"? Explain.

4. Does emphasis on God's law carry the danger of forgetting God's grace? Explain.

5. Do you agree that God's law can serve as a resource for mission? Explain.

SMALL GROUP SESSION IDEAS

Opening (10-15 minutes)

Pray/Worship—Open with a prayer of gratitude for each person in the group and for the privilege of studying God's Word together. Ask the Holy Spirit to guide your session and your daily living.

You might also wish to read the first stanza of Psalm 119 (vv. 1-8) and make a regular practice of reading a stanza of this psalm each time you gather for this study.

If your group likes to sing, you could also include music at this time by singing "Guide Me, O My Great Redeemer" or another inspiring hymn about living the Christian life.

Share—Your group leader will have some comments to share with you as you begin this study of the Ten Commandments together.

Focus—As you move through the lesson, consider focusing on the following question: *When I hear God say, "Choose life," how can I respond on a daily basis?*

Growing (35-40 minutes)

Read (optional)—Most groups benefit from reading the Scripture passage each time they gather. Along with your group leader, figure out which way(s) you as a group might best read Scripture together.

Discuss—In addition to the General Discussion questions provided, you may wish to reflect on and respond to some of the following:

- Think of some people in your life who have taught or shown you how to live. Did they teach you the best way to live? Did they teach you habits or perspectives that you have to unlearn? Share your thoughts with the rest of the group, if you're comfortable doing so.
- Are you more tempted to legalism or to license (lawlessness)? In other words, are you tempted to act more like the

prodigal son or the prodigal's brother? (See Luke 15:11-32.) Explain.

- Could you, as Paul did, tell people, "Follow my example, as I follow the example of Christ" (1 Cor. 11:1)? Explain.

Goalsetting (5 minutes)

One specific goal to start off with could be to learn the Ten Commandments by heart as given in Exodus 20 or Deuteronomy 5, or you could learn an abbreviated version that states the essence of each command. If you already know the commandments by heart, considering memorizing Psalm 1.

Another goal could be to begin or renew mealtime devotions in your household. For example, you could begin by saying, "Four, five, or six times this week, we will read a passage from the Bible and pray after our evening meal." If you accomplish this every day, congratulations! Or perhaps you need to develop a habit of daily personal devotions. Whatever the case, set a realistic goal, ask God for help with it, and get going!

Closing (10-15 minutes)

Preparing for Prayer—As you prepare for prayer at the close of each session, think about including personal praises and petitions in your prayer together. Think also about your life in light of the lesson material. (For example, you could thank God for something you've learned during this lesson, and you could pray for an opportunity to teach the good news of Jesus or a Bible lesson to someone else in a way that combines learning with witness.)

Before praying, you might like to read the Beatitudes (Matt. 5:3-12) as a reminder of God's grace that precedes God's instructions for living (see Matt. 5:13-7:29). Or you could just read the first beatitude: "Blessed are the poor in spirit, for theirs is the kingdom of heaven" (Matt. 5:3).

Prayer—Thank God for the opportunity you've had to begin studying the Ten Commandments together, and ask the Holy Spirit for help each day in applying what you've learned about the *torah,* God's mission, and the first commandment. You may join in with personal petitions and praises, if you like. You may also wish to include a time of silence for personal confession and private prayer. Then end your prayer with some closing words or perhaps a verse or two from Scripture, such as, "Search me, O God, and know my heart; test me and know my anxious thoughts. See if there is any offensive way in me, and lead me in the way everlasting" (Ps. 139:23-24).

Group Project/Study Goal (Optional)

Members of Jewish congregations sometimes form what they call "mitzvah" groups, or they come up with "mitzvah" projects. "Mitzvah" comes from the Hebrew word for "commandment," and, in this context, it means doing a good deed. As individuals or as a group, you could plan various "mitzvahs" that you could carry out in the coming weeks. For example, you could do yard work or some other project for seniors in your church or neighbors of your church community, or you might consider leading a worship service in a nursing home, or driving someone around to do their shopping. Come up with your own creative ideas—from the heart!

How shall we worship?

2

DEUTERONOMY 5:8-10; EXODUS 32:1-8, 19-20; 34:1-10

True Worship

In a Nutshell

The second commandment forbids graven images and all forms of idolatry (Deut. 5:8-10). More specifically, it prohibits wrong or corrupted worship. Positively, this commandment calls us to know the one true God and to worship the Lord in a way that acknowledges God's character. Israel's worship of the golden calf gives us insight into the nature of idolatry. The Lord's covenant renewal offers guidance for true worship.

Deuteronomy 5:8-10

8"You shall not make for yourself an idol in the form of anything in heaven above or on the earth beneath or in the waters below. 9You shall not bow down to them or worship them; for I, the LORD your God, am a jealous God, punishing the children for the sin of the fathers to the third and fourth generation of those who hate me, 10but showing love to a thousand generations of those who love me and keep my commandments."

Exodus 32:1-8, 19-20

1When the people saw that Moses was so long in coming down from the mountain, they gathered around Aaron and said, "Come, make us gods who will go before us. As for this fellow Moses who brought us up out of Egypt, we don't know what has happened to him."

2Aaron answered them, "Take off the gold earrings that your wives, your sons and your daughters are wearing, and bring them to me." 3So all the people took off their earrings and brought them to Aaron. 4He took what they handed him and made it into an idol cast in the shape of a calf, fashioning it with a tool. Then they said, "These are your gods, O Israel, who brought you up out of Egypt."

5When Aaron saw this, he built an altar in front of the calf and announced, "Tomorrow there will be a festival to the LORD." 6So the next day the people rose early and sacrificed burnt offerings and presented fellowship offerings. Afterward they sat down to eat and drink and got up to indulge in revelry.

7Then the LORD said to Moses, "Go down, because your people, whom you brought up out of Egypt, have become corrupt. 8They have been quick to turn away from what I commanded them and have made themselves an idol cast in the shape of a calf. They have bowed down to it and sacrificed to it and have said, 'These are your gods, O Israel, who brought you up out of Egypt.'" . . .

19When Moses approached the camp and saw the calf and the dancing, his anger burned and he threw the tablets [inscribed by God] out of his hands, breaking them to pieces at the foot of the mountain. 20And he took the calf they had made and burned it in the fire; then he ground it to powder, scattered it on the water and made the Israelites drink it.

34:1-10

1The LORD said to Moses, "Chisel out two stone tablets like the first ones, and I will write on them the words that were on the first tablets, which you broke. 2Be ready in the morning, and then come up on Mount Sinai. Present yourself to me there on top of the mountain. 3No one is to come with you or be seen anywhere on the mountain; not even the flocks and herds may graze in front of the mountain."

4So Moses chiseled out two stone tablets like the first ones and went up Mount Sinai early in the morning, as the LORD had commanded him; and he carried the two stone tablets in his hands. 5Then the LORD came down in the cloud and stood there with him and proclaimed his name, the LORD. 6And he passed in front of Moses, proclaiming, "The LORD, the LORD, the compassionate and gracious God, slow to anger, abounding in love and faithfulness, 7maintaining love to thousands, and forgiving wickedness, rebellion and sin. Yet he does not leave the guilty unpunished; he punishes the children and their children for the sin of the fathers to the third and fourth generation."

8Moses bowed to the ground at once and worshiped. 9"O Lord, if I have found favor in your eyes," he said, "then let the Lord go with us. Although this is a stiff-necked people, forgive our wickedness and our sin, and take us as your inheritance."

10Then the LORD said: "I am making a covenant with you. Before all your people I will do wonders never before done in any nation in all the world. The people you live among will see how awesome is the work that I, the LORD, will do for you.

Theology Matters

Philip Yancey describes visiting a church in Indiana. The service centered on Bible study, and it was attended by many traditional families. Yancey could see that the parents in these families loved their children. But he also knew that some of these very parents had, without seeking any medical help, watched their children grow sick and die. One father had watched his infant son become deaf and then blind and finally die. The child's disease was a treatable form of meningitis, but this father, instructed by his pastor, believed that faith in God meant refusing to call a doctor. In his book *Disappointment with God* Yancey writes, "I went away from that Sunday service with a profound conviction that what we think about God and believe about God matters—really matters—as much as anything in life matters."

Covenant Rupture

In the story of the golden calf, the people of Israel think about God and engage in vigorous religious activity. Under the leadership of Aaron, they hold "a festival to the LORD" that includes sacrifices and fellowship offerings (Ex. 32:5). Their worship, however, violates both the first and second commandments, and the result is a nearly fatal rupture in their covenantal relationship with God.

The narrative indicates Israel's violation of the second commandment in at least two ways. Notice the description of the making of an idol in the form of a calf, and note also the use of the verbs "made" and "bowed down" in Exodus 32:8. These verbs clearly echo the wording of the second commandment—not to mention that the Lord points out, "They have been quick to turn away from what I commanded them" (32:8; see chap. 24).

We can note further that Israel at the same time violates the first commandment. This display gives us a clear example of how closely the first and second commandments are related. While Aaron claims to plan "a festival to the LORD" (32:5), his fashioning of a calf reveals that he has actually brought another god alongside the one true God. In the ancient Middle East, calves and bulls symbolized divine strength that pagan peoples sought from their various gods. So even though Aaron speaks in the name of "the LORD," his use of this pagan symbol leads the people to turn to "other gods" (Ex. 20:3; Deut. 5:7). This comes out when the people say, "These are your gods, O Israel, who brought you up out of Egypt" (Ex. 32:4).

Idolatrous worship, even when offered in the name of the one true God, results in bowing down to a false god. The fruit of this twisted worship can be seen in the indulgent revelry that follows (32:6). Evildoing flows from corrupt worship; immorality flows from idolatry. The result of this worship is a covenant that is as broken as the two tablets Moses later breaks at the foot of Mount Sinai (32:19).

It's important to note here that Israel cloaks its violation of the covenant in religious activity and lip service to the Lord. Cloaking disobedience in the garb of religion goes back to the serpent's temptation of God's people in Eden. The serpent did not attempt a direct denial of God and God's authority. Instead, the serpent engaged in theological speculation by asking, "Did God really say . . . ?" (Gen. 3:1). The religious character of idolatry implies the importance of true worship, sound doctrine, and Bible study. But as Yancey's story teaches, and as the story of the golden calf reveals, wrong worship and wrong thinking about God can lead to death. The only antidote is true worship and sound teachings.

Covenant Renewal

Israel's idolatrous worship of the golden calf is all the more pathetic when we compare it to God's self-revelation in Exodus 34. In this passage God symbolizes the renewal of the broken covenant by commanding Moses: "Chisel out two stone tablets like the first ones . . . which you broke" (34:1). Moses then witnesses the revelation of God's true and essential self. First comes the pronouncement of God's covenantal name, "The LORD, the LORD." Then God interprets this name by explaining God's character: "the compassionate and gracious God, slow to anger, abounding in love and faithfulness, maintaining love to thousands, and forgiving wickedness, rebellion, and sin" (34:6-7). This is who God really is; this is what God is truly like.

God's self-revelation here is one of the great moments in the history of salvation and, therefore, in the history of the world. Had God been less compassionate and gracious, God could have sentenced the Israelites to death. Instead, "the LORD" so abounds in covenantal love and faithfulness as to forgive the people's rebellion.

But notice the hint that such grace to sinners is costly when God reveals the requirement of justice, saying, "Yet he does not leave the guilty unpunished" (34:7). God speaks here of punishing "the children and their children for the sin of the fathers" (34:7). In time, as Christians know, Christ would fulfill this passage by embodying God's "grace and truth" as God's "One and Only" Son (John 1:14), effectively taking "away the sin of the world" (1:29). The God who loved the world enough to send this Son not "to condemn the world, but to save the world through him" (3:17) reveals the same passionate determination to save by grace already here at Sinai. God's gracious salvation flows from God's gracious character. And all who come to know the true God's character by authentic worship can rejoice in this salvation.

"Worship Wars" or Intercessory Prayer

One way to connect both the second commandment and Exodus 32-34 to the mission of the church is to compare Moses' intercession to "worship wars" that congregations have often waged in the name of true worship and outreach.

The golden calf episode reveals that we should take worship seriously. We should not accommodate worship to the pagan spirit of our age in ways that lead to idolatry and death. For example, we should not confuse worship with entertainment. To do this offends God and promotes death. However, while maintaining standards for worship, we should not be led by a gracelessness that fails to reflect God's compassion for sinners.

Instead of these two false ways, we can carry out worship in a way that reflects God's character. In our preaching, prayers, and entire liturgy, we can strive to acknowledge the holy otherness of God, and at the same time we can acknowledge that this is the same God who is compassionate and gracious to sinners. Debates about traditional versus contemporary forms of worship should be subordinate to the essence of worship, which is an encounter between "the compassionate and gracious God" (Ex. 34:6) and the sinful people who "are the kind of worshipers the Father seeks" (John 4:23). When we disagree about the forms for encountering this gracious God, we can pray for each other the way Moses prayed for Israel (Ex. 34:9). Our worship should be such that when seekers say, "we would like to see Jesus" (John 12:21), they will meet the Lord through believers who live and worship in God's presence, embodying these words of Jesus: "Anyone who has seen me has seen the Father" (14:9).

Additional Notes

32:1—The Israelites say, "Come, make us gods." The word for "gods" here is *elohim,* which can be translated both by the words "a god" and by the word "God." We translate *elohim* as "God" when it is used in reference to the one true God.

"This fellow Moses who brought us up out of Egypt." With these words, the Israelites manage both to attribute the exodus to Moses rather than to the Lord, and to insult Moses. This fickleness and confusion reveal their desperate need for divine formation and instruction by means of true worship.

32:2-4—Later in Israelite history, Gideon repeated Aaron's error of asking the Israelites to donate earrings, which he melted down and made into an object of worship—an ephod, which "became a snare to Gideon and his family" (see Judg. 8:24-27). Still later, Jeroboam led the northern kingdom of Israel astray by setting up golden calves and saying, "Here are your gods, O Israel, who brought you up out of Egypt" (1 Kings 12:28). Idolatry is a continual temptation for God's people.

32:6—"to indulge in revelry." This phrase carries overtones of sexual immorality, which was often a part of pagan religious festivals in the ancient Middle East.

34:3—God allows "no one . . . to come with" Moses. At the earlier covenant confirmation described in Exodus 24, Aaron and other Israelite leaders were included in a way that is not repeated here. This change implies a rebuke for their failure to lead responsibly during Moses' earlier time on Mount Sinai.

34:6-7—God's self-revelation here is a response to Moses' request in 33:13 to "know" (that is, to "gain intimate, experiential knowledge of") the Lord. God's "glory" (33:18) is revealed as God comes down "in the cloud" and proclaims "his name, the LORD" (34:5).

GENERAL DISCUSSION

1. How would you describe the sin of Aaron? Why is Aaron's sin so serious?

2. Why does idolatry lead to immorality?

3. What is the antidote to idolatry and immorality?

4. What steps can you take to promote knowledge of the Lord as revealed in Exodus 34:6-7?

SMALL GROUP SESSION IDEAS

Opening (10-15 minutes)

Pray/Worship—As you open this session with prayer, begin by praising the Lord as the "compassionate and gracious God, slow to anger, abounding in love and faithfulness" (Ex. 34:6). Ask God the Holy Spirit to guide you as you discuss the second commandment together, and pray that you may have open hearts to hear and learn from God's words for your lives.

You could also read Psalm 103 together, or follow along as your group leader reads the psalm out loud.

If you enjoy singing, "Amazing Grace" would be fitting at this point in your session.

Share—Discuss briefly what you think of the point in lesson 1 about God's law equipping believers for God's mission. What issues do you think are most controversial when congregations decide to emphasize mission and evangelism?

Focus—Throughout this session try focusing on the following question: *Does the way I worship and live reflect God's character?*

Growing (35-40 minutes)

Read (optional)—If you'd like to read the Scripture passages for this lesson before moving into your discussion time, perhaps two or three of you could read those passages for the rest of the group. After reading the Exodus 34 passage, go back and reread 34:6 to emphasize the revelation of God's name and character.

Discuss—In addition to the General Discussion questions, you may want to reflect on and talk about some of the following process questions:

- On what do I base my views of worship? Do I think more about my personal tastes or the character of God?
- How do I view God? Do I see God as deeply disappointed in me, or do I see God as someone who views me with compassion and grace? Do I see God as revealed most perfectly in Jesus Christ?
- Do I take God's grace for granted and, therefore, cheapen it? How can I remind myself regularly of the amazing character of God's grace?
- Do I prepare myself for worship services?
- Do I pray for my enemies in the church and outside of it?

Goalsetting (5 minutes)

Learning the Ten Commandments by heart, getting into mealtime or personal devotions, or forming a "mitzvah" group, as suggested in session 1, are all ongoing projects that you could review as you think about goalsetting during this session.

If you're ready to move on in terms of goalsetting, you may wish to memorize Exodus 34:6-7 or Psalm 103. You might also consider beginning a prayer diary for recording prayers of gratitude, confession, and intercession.

Closing (10-15 minutes)

Preparing for Prayer—In addition to sharing joys and concerns within your group, you could think about ways to intercede for your congregation(s).

Prayer—If you haven't read Psalm 103 already, you could do so now as the beginning of your prayer. Everyone should feel free to join in with joys, concerns, and intercessions. Pray also that through the church's worship and mission, the character of God may become known to all peoples. For a sung prayer that you could use as your closing, try "Praise, My Soul, the King of Heaven."

Group Intercession Project (Optional)

Consider committing to intercessory prayer during the coming week. You could promise to pray for each other or for someone in your church or for someone you know who is having a particularly tough time.

Why do we say,
"Lord, Lord?"

3

DEUTERONOMY 5:11; LEVITICUS 24:10-23

In the Name of the Lord

In a Nutshell

The third commandment prohibits "misuse [of] the name of the Lord" (Deut. 5:11). Our misuse of God's name is not limited to cursing or swearing that turns God's name into foul language. This commandment has to do with misrepresenting God (and thus maligning God's character) in any context. Positively, the third commandment calls us to speak and live in a way that reflects God's holiness. In all we say and do, God's good name and reputation are at stake.

The disturbing story about a blasphemer in Leviticus 24 reminds us forcefully of a central truth that we easily forget in today's populist, relativistic society: *the Lord our God is holy.* In light of the good news in Jesus Christ, the point of the story is not to advocate death for blasphemers but to urge us to a holiness that energizes us to reflect God's character to everyone around us.

Deuteronomy 5:11

"You shall not misuse the name of the Lord your God, for the Lord will not hold anyone guiltless who misuses his name."

Leviticus 24:10-23

10Now the son of an Israelite mother
and an Egyptian father went out among
the Israelites, and a fight broke out in the
camp between him and an Israelite. 11The
son of the Israelite woman blasphemed
the Name with a curse; so they brought
him to Moses. (His mother's name was
Shelomith, the daughter of Dibri the
Danite.) 12They put him in custody until
the will of the Lord should be made clear
to them.
13Then the Lord said to Moses: 14"Take
the blasphemer outside the camp. All
those who heard him are to lay their
hands on his head, and the entire assembly is to stone him. 15Say to the Israelites:
'If anyone curses his God, he will be held
responsible; 16anyone who blasphemes
the name of the Lord must be put to
death. The entire assembly must stone
him. Whether an alien or native-born,
when he blasphemes the Name, he must
be put to death.

17"'If anyone takes the life of a human
being, he must be put to death. 18Anyone
who takes the life of someone's animal
must make restitution—life for life. 19If
anyone injures his neighbor, whatever he
has done must be done to him: 20fracture
for fracture, eye for eye, tooth for tooth. As
he has injured the other, so he is to be
injured. 21Whoever kills an animal must
make restitution, but whoever kills a man
must be put to death. 22You are to have the
same law for the alien and the native-
born. I am the LORD your God.'"

23Then Moses spoke to the Israelites,
and they took the blasphemer outside the
camp and stoned him. The Israelites did as
the LORD commanded Moses.

Additional reading: Hebrews 10:19-31

"Ugh"

Imagine that you have finally persuaded some unbelieving friends to join you in worshiping God on a Sunday morning. Then imagine the minister reading Leviticus 24:10-23 as the basis for the sermon that day. How comfortable would your friends feel in relation to this passage? How comfortable would you feel?

Early in the provocative novel *The Brothers K,* author David James Duncan portrays a young boy passing time by flipping through the Bible at random. First he comes across 1 Samuel 22 and reads about Doeg the Edomite slaughtering eighty-five priests. The next passage he finds also involves shocking brutality. The boy's reaction to these biblical stories is "Ugh."

Some people could react to the stoning of the blasphemer in Leviticus 24 in the same way. Even people who revere the Bible might wonder what to make of this harsh story. In the heat of a fight, a man blasphemes the name of the Lord. Does that merit the death penalty?

God as Fire

We may never become comfortable with this story, but we can begin to make sense of it if we see it in the context of the Lord's covenant with Israel at Sinai. At Mount Sinai the Lord God, who has defeated Pharaoh and made all the nations tremble (see Ex. 14-15), descends with a display of lightning, thunder, a thick cloud, and a trumpet blast that makes the children of Israel tremble (19:16). As the Lord descends to the top of the mountain, the people are warned not to come too close. They also "must consecrate themselves, or the LORD will break out against them" (19:22).

Such precautions are necessary because it is dangerous for sinful people to meet a holy God. God's holiness gives us a sense of God's otherness from every creature. God's holiness is most sharply recognized in view of God's separation from sin.

The otherness and purity of God make God dangerous to sinners who approach in a careless way. We cannot treat God lightly and live. "To the Israelites the glory of the LORD looked like a consuming fire on top of the mountain" (24:17).

In the *torah,* and especially in Leviticus, the fiery God of Sinai instructs the people in holiness so that the Lord can dwell among them without consuming them (see 29:42-46; 40:34-38). This is the context in which the incident in Leviticus 24 takes place. God's meeting with the people at Sinai is a crucial moment in the history of Israel and, therefore, in the history of the world. The holy Lord is forming Israel into a holy people. At such a time the Lord does not seek to make us comfortable. God insists on the sanctity of his name in a memorable way. So after "Moses spoke to the Israelites," they "took the blasphemer outside the camp and stoned him. The Israelites did as the LORD commanded Moses" (Lev. 24:23).

Hallowed Be God's Name

The theme of God's holiness is not limited to the book of Leviticus or to the Old Testament. The writer of Hebrews, for example, even when contrasting our coming to God through Jesus with Israel's coming to Sinai, insists that God is holy (Heb. 10:22, 26-31). "Therefore, since we are receiving a kingdom that cannot be shaken, let us be thankful, and so worship God acceptably with reverence and awe, for our 'God is a consuming fire'" (12:28-29; see Deut. 4:24). The coming of Christ does not render God's dangerous holiness obsolete, as some people are inclined to think. Instead, the coming of Christ displays God's holiness in a new way.

In the gospel of Mark, for example, an unclean spirit identifies Jesus as "the Holy One of God" (Mark 1:24). Jesus displays the power of God's holiness by rebuking and casting out the unclean spirit. But Jesus performs this act of power for the sake of healing a possessed man. Holiness as healing power becomes a central theme in Jesus' mission. When Jesus meets a leper—someone identified as "unclean" according to the holiness code—Jesus is filled with compassion, touches the man, and heals him (1:40-42). In relation to all who are sick with sin, Jesus expresses God's holiness as a healing presence (see 2:15-17).

When we recognize Jesus' commitment to holiness for life and salvation, we can begin to understand why he gives top priority to God's holiness in the Lord's Prayer. The very first and governing petition of the Lord's Prayer is "Hallowed be your name" (Matt. 6:9). God's holiness, combined with the rest of God's attributes as signified by God's name, serves as the fountainhead for the coming of God's kingdom, the doing of God's will, the provision of daily bread and all other necessities, the forgiveness of sins, and deliverance from the evil one (6:10-13). Only the Holy One has the power to save sinners from the evil one.

Jesus' reverence for the book of Leviticus, with its theme of holiness, comes out in his summary of the law *(torah)*. According to Jesus, we can sum up "the Law and the Prophets" with two passages: one from Deuteronomy 6:5 ("Love the Lord your God with all your heart . . ."—see lesson 1) and the other from Leviticus 19:18 ("Love your neighbor as yourself"—see Matt. 22:37-40). Jesus' instructions on prayer and love indicate that only those who "take time to be holy" will have the God-given energy to love God and their neighbors.

Training for Mission

In his "Letter from a Birmingham Jail," Martin Luther King, Jr., describes the training steps he and other civil rights activists took in order to prepare for nonviolent protests against the evil power of segregation. He calls step 3 "self-purification" and explains that he and his colleagues established workshops in which they repeatedly asked themselves, "Are you able to accept blows without retaliating? Are you able to endure the ordeals of jail?" Only after going through this Lenten-like time of spiritual exercise were they able to launch their direct-action campaign with any hope toward combining integrity with accomplishment.

If the need for self-purification, or exercises in holiness, applies to a civil rights mission, it applies also to the Christian mission of spreading the good news and witnessing to the character of God's kingdom. If we use the Lord's name and are called by the name Christian and yet fail to reflect what those names mean, we drive people away from God. As commentator Terence Fretheim observes, "The name of God is so commonly associated with empty phrases or easy religion or the latest ideology of a social or political sort . . . [that it] gets dragged down to the level of the contexts in which it is used." Negative associations with the name of God can encourage people to avoid or reject God.

On the other hand, the proper use of God's name in our praise and holy living can draw people toward the Lord. Fretheim points to such passages as Psalms 48:10 and 86:9 and concludes, "God's mission for the world is linked to the use of the divine name."

Additional Notes

Lev. 24:10—"the son of . . . an Egyptian father." The *NIV Study Bible* rightly relates this detail not to bigotry against foreigners but to the consistent and equal application of God's law to both aliens and native-born Israelites (see 24:22).

The word for "fight" in this verse refers to a physical fight.

24:11—Biblical reverence for God's name can be seen in the narrator's reference simply to "the Name." The offender blasphemed by pronouncing the Lord's name as a curse. The narrator apparently stands at a distance from the offense by refusing to use the phrase "the Name of the LORD" or "the Name of God."

Compare with the story in the book of Job, where Job's wife says, "Curse God and die!" (Job 2:9). As David Noel Freedman points out in his book *The Nine Commandments,* "In Hebrew, Job's wife literally exclaims, '*Bless* God and die.'" The biblical narrator apparently refuses even to write the words "Curse God," but it's clear from the context that this is what Job's wife actually urges Job to do. So translators correctly render the verse as we find it in our Bibles. (See also Job 2:5.)

24:14—Commentator Baruch A. Levine explains that capital sentences were executed "outside the camp" for reasons "due, at least in part, to the impurity attached to a corpse." In addition to noting this holiness theme, Levine also points out that taking a human life, even when done with proper judicial procedure, was seen "as a horrendous act." This observation validates our humanitarian questions about this passage.

24:15—The requirement that "the entire assembly" stone the blasphemer brings out the communal character of biblical holiness and responsibility.

24:20—The specification "fracture for fracture, eye for eye" is related to the general principles of restitution and proportionality in punishment. This expression of what is often called the *lex talionis,* or "law of retaliation" (see also Ex. 21:23-25; Deut. 19:21), is meant not to promote revenge but instead to prevent spiraling cycles of violence. It limits rather than escalates violence and puts potential feuds under the restraints of judicial procedure. In the context of newly reconstituted Israel, who had only recently been freed from more than 400 years of slavery and oppression, this law is a step toward humane expressions of justice.

We can see how this is true when we consider that our sinful inclination is to hit back harder or cause more damage to someone who has hurt us or caused us trouble. The law calls the people to step back from that position and, rather than striking back in anger and adding to the offense, to give it over to the law to be dealt with by the community according to God's commands.

The Lord Jesus urges us, further, to take the next step toward forgiveness when he says, "You have heard that it was said, 'Eye for eye, and tooth for tooth.' But I tell you, Do not resist an evil person. If someone strikes you on the right cheek, turn to him the other also. . . . You have heard that it was said, 'Love your neighbor and hate your enemy.' But I tell you: Love your enemies and pray for those who persecute you" (Matt. 5:38-39, 43-44).

GENERAL DISCUSSION

1. Reflect on how the story from Leviticus 24 affects you. Would this be a good passage to read in a worship service? Explain.

2. When you hear the word *holy,* what comes to mind? How does Jesus shape your understanding of holiness?

3. How familiar are you with the book of Leviticus? What makes Leviticus worth reading?

4. What do people think of when they hear the word *Christian?*

SMALL GROUP SESSION IDEAS

Opening (10-15 minutes)

Pray/Worship—As you open with prayer for this session, you could pray Psalm 99 or incorporate it into your prayer.

If you like to sing, "Creator Spirit, by Whose Aid" could serve as an opening hymn.

Share—If some or all of you have begun projects or set goals, share how these things are going.

Focus—During this session, keep in mind the mercy of God connected with the revelation of God's name (from lesson 2) and think about how this fits with God's holiness in connection with God's name. Focus by asking, *How do God's mercy and holiness go together?*

Growing (35-40 minutes)

Read (optional)—You may wish to read the Scripture passages for this lesson (as well as portions of the lesson notes) before moving into your discussion time.

Discuss—As you cover the General Discussion questions, you may wish to include some or all of the following process questions:

- Do I "take time to be holy?" When and how?
- How do I start my days—with TV, radio, or prayer?
- What does the petition "Hallowed be your name" mean to me?
- How can we be holy without becoming "holier than thou"? How can the example of Jesus help us here?

Goalsetting (5 minutes)

You may wish to continue learning Scripture passages by heart, adding Psalm 29 or Isaiah 6:1-8 to your memory work.

Or, by this time in your study, you may have become aware of an area in which you've fallen and need to ask for God's forgiveness and renewal. If so, you may wish to set a goal that helps you commit to more and more faithfully reflecting God's holiness, mercy, and mission through your life.

Closing (10-15 minutes)

Preparing for Prayer—Spend some time together mentioning personal prayer concerns and praises, as well as goals and projects you may be working on in connection with your study of the Ten Commandments.

As you prepare for prayer, you could also focus on God's holiness and mission with a reading of Isaiah 6:1-8.

Prayer—Thank the one holy God that in Christ you can approach the Lord in confidence as you bring confessions, concerns, and praises to the throne of grace. Everyone may join in with items they'd like to mention, and perhaps observe a time of silence for confession and other private matters. Ask the covenant Lord for wisdom in living so that each of you can faithfully reflect God's holiness and mission in all you do.

Group Project (Optional)

To bring out the socially dynamic quality of holiness, you may want to consider some kind of training and witness that echoes the civil rights training of Martin Luther King, Jr. You could begin by reading King's "Letter from a Birmingham Jail" in *Blessed Are the Peacemakers* by S. Jonathan Bass (Baton Rouge: Louisiana State University Press, 2001) and then seeing how King's training steps might be applied to deal with important issues today.

For additional training in holiness, you could also consult books by Richard J. Foster, such as *Celebration of Discipline: The Path to Spiritual Growth* (San Francisco: Harper & Row, 1988) and *Devotional Classics: Selected Readings for Individuals and Groups,* ed. Richard J. Foster and James Bryan Smith (San Francisco: HarperSanFrancisco, 1993).

Whom will you serve?

4

DEUTERONOMY 5:12-15; MATTHEW 11:25-12:14

The Yoke That Fits

In a Nutshell

In the fourth commandment the Lord urges us to "remember" (Ex. 20:8) or to "observe the Sabbath day" (Deut. 5:11). Jesus observes this positive command by doing good. He heals and works for human beings in order to give them the life that comes from his heavenly Father. Negatively, the Sabbath commandment calls us to rest from our own sinful ways. The practice of discipleship guides us in both the positive and negative aspects of this controversial commandment.

Deuteronomy 5:12-15

12"Observe the Sabbath day by keeping it holy, as the LORD your God has commanded you. 13Six days you shall labor and do all your work, 14but the seventh day is a Sabbath to the LORD your God. On it you shall not do any work, neither you, nor your son or daughter, nor your manservant or maidservant, nor your ox, your donkey or any of your animals, nor the alien within your gates, so that your manservant and maidservant may rest, as you do. 15Remember that you were slaves in Egypt and that the LORD your God brought you out of there with a mighty hand and an outstretched arm. Therefore the LORD your God has commanded you to observe the Sabbath day."

Matthew 11:25-30

25. . . Jesus said, "I praise you, Father, Lord of heaven and earth, because you have hidden these things from the wise and learned, and revealed them to little children. 26Yes, Father, for this was your good pleasure.

27"All things have been committed to me by my Father. No one knows the Son except the Father, and no one knows the Father except the Son and those to whom the Son chooses to reveal him.

28"Come to me, all you who are weary and burdened, and I will give you rest. 29Take my yoke upon you and learn from me, for I am gentle and humble in heart, and you will find rest for your souls. 30For my yoke is easy and my burden is light."

12:1-14

1At that time Jesus went through the grainfields on the Sabbath. His disciples were hungry and began to pick some heads of grain and eat them. 2When the Pharisees saw this, they said to him, "Look! Your disciples are doing what is unlawful on the Sabbath."

3He answered, "Haven't you read what
David did when he and his companions
were hungry? 4He entered the house of
God, and he and his companions ate the
consecrated bread—which was not lawful
for them to do, but only for the priests. 5Or
haven't you read in the Law that on the
Sabbath the priests in the temple desecrate
the day and yet are innocent? 6I tell you
that one greater than the temple is here.
7If you had known what these words
mean, 'I desire mercy, not sacrifice,' you
would not have condemned the innocent.
8For the Son of Man is Lord of the
Sabbath."

9Going on from that place, he went
into their synagogue, 10and a man with a
shriveled hand was there. Looking for a
reason to accuse Jesus, they asked him, "Is
it lawful to heal on the Sabbath?"

11He said to them, "If any of you has a
sheep and it falls into a pit on the Sabbath,
will you not take hold of it and lift it out?
12How much more valuable is a man than
a sheep! Therefore it is lawful to do good
on the Sabbath."

13Then he said to the man, "Stretch out
your hand." So he stretched it out and it
was completely restored, just as sound as
the other. 14But the Pharisees went out
and plotted how they might kill Jesus.

Who Is Pharaoh Today?

Recently I read a newspaper article about what economists call the "24-7" economy. In this setting the goal is for goods and services to be available 24 hours a day, 7 days a week. Inevitably, such a goal requires people to work long hours every day, including Saturday and Sunday. The article concluded by asking whether the 24-7 economy was a good development or a bad one.

Believers can begin to answer that question by recalling Moses' first interview with Pharaoh in Egypt. When Moses told Pharaoh that God had said, "Let my people go, so that they may hold a festival to me in the desert," Pharaoh refused by asking, with contempt, "Who is the Lord, that I should obey him?" (Ex. 5:1-2). Pharaoh then required the Israelites to make bricks without giving them the straw needed to make them, and when they complained, Pharaoh said, "Lazy, that's what you are—lazy! That is why you keep saying, 'Let us go and sacrifice to the Lord.' Now get to work. You will not be given any straw, yet you must produce your full quota of bricks" (5:17-18). Pharaoh would have approved of a 24-7 economy, at least in regard to his slave laborers.

As believers, we need to ask ourselves, *To what extent do we do the same? And what does it (or should it) mean to observe the Sabbath as Christians with an eye toward entering God's Sabbath rest?* (See Heb. 4.) Often our habits of work and consumption are little different from those of unbelievers, and they threaten to enslave us to the schedules of a 24-7 economy. Have we allowed the market to become our Pharaoh? Have we enslaved ourselves to the market to the point of becoming our own Pharaohs?

The Lord of the Sabbath Offers Rest

In Matthew 12 Jesus and the Pharisees dispute the proper way to observe the Sabbath. For some Christians, the accusatory (Matt. 12:2) and ultimately murderous (12:14) attitude of the Pharisees brings up bad memories of Sabbath legalism that they experienced in church (and church-related) communities. Any faith tradition that takes God's law seriously is tempted to fall into legalism, and many faith traditions have been guilty of legalism on the matter of Sunday observance. It's sad that in the name of Jesus Christians have sometimes acted like Jesus' opponents with respect to the Sabbath. They have frowned on almost any activity that could make Sunday into a day of joy.

If we are right to reject such legalistic interpretations of the Sabbath, however, we are wrong if we think the Sabbath did not matter to Jesus at all. Jesus proclaims himself "Lord of the Sabbath" (12:8), and, as such, he fulfills the Sabbath in a way that brings mercy, healing, and other good gifts from God. Jesus shows mercy by allowing his hungry disciples to pick grain on the Sabbath. He restores health to a man's shriveled hand. He also offers a general guideline, stating, "It is lawful to do good on the Sabbath" (12:12).

Pharisaic judgmentalism about the Sabbath is not healthy, but neither is consumeristic greed that ignores Jesus' own observance of the Sabbath. We do not follow Jesus by working or playing till we drop from exhaustion. We follow Jesus by living in spiritual freedom, showing mercy, bringing healing, and finding creative ways to serve God with an eye toward Sabbath rest on Sunday and every other day.

One practice that can set us free to do good is to rest from our own self-centered pursuits in order to rest in God. Such Sabbath practices should actually apply to everyday living, but they can also apply to our Sunday living in a special way. By listening to God and enjoying communion with God's people, we can anticipate and enter even now into the "Sabbath-rest [that remains] for the people of God" (Heb. 4:9). As we think about this, we need to bear in mind that in the Scriptures rest is not boring inactivity or laziness. Rest is refreshment in God that comes from trust in and obedience to God. Jesus' glad miracles of healing on the Jewish Sabbath are previews of the refreshment and joy that wait for all of us who trust and obey him.

Whose Yoke?

As an alternative to both Sabbath legalism and slavery to money in a 24-7 economy, we can gain insight from the passage that comes just before the Sabbath controversy in Matthew 12. At the end of Matthew 11, Jesus invites us to enter his rest by following him as disciples. Jesus calls us to discipleship by saying, "Take my yoke upon you and learn from me" (Matt. 11:29).

In those days, to wear someone's yoke was to submit to and serve under that person's authority (see Jer. 27-28). Jesus promises that if we serve and learn from him rather than from other masters, he will give us rest. We will not, for example, exhaust ourselves by running like unbelievers after material security (see Matt. 6:32). We will not have anxiety about salvation or fear anyone or anything except "the One who can destroy both soul and body in hell"—and who actually is our loving heavenly Father (10:26-31). Following Jesus' teachings about these and all things allows us to "find rest for [our] souls" (11:29). Jesus explains, "For my yoke is easy and my burden is light" (11:30).

Discipleship and Growth

The fourth commandment as fulfilled by Jesus has led us to recognize discipleship as the life-giving alternative to both legalism and license (or the rejection of all restraints). The practice of discipleship can guide us not only regarding Sabbath rest but also regarding the church's mission in general. In a world in which many people are "weary and burdened" (11:28), we can present Jesus as the One who teaches us to live joyfully now. Jesus' rest and his everlasting life last forever, but they begin already in this life for all who follow him as disciples.

In his excellent book on discipleship, *The Divine Conspiracy,* Dallas Willard emphasizes learning from Jesus and teaching others to follow Jesus as an effective biblical alternative to the consumeristic mindset that infects so many evangelistic efforts today. Willard calls mission in the form of discipleship "church growth for those who hate it." By this he means that we can evangelize without "dumbing down" or watering down the gospel in any way. We can evangelize by making disciples who live with a view toward God's ultimate Sabbath rest every day. And in this mission Jesus promises to be with us "always, to the very end of the age" (Matt. 28:20).

Additional Notes

Matt. 11:28—Of the four gospel accounts, Matthew alone includes Jesus' call to discipleship in this form. The gracious character of discipleship comes through especially in Jesus' kind words "Come to me, all you who are weary and burdened. . . ." If we serve other masters, they will burden us. If we serve Jesus, he will give us "rest."

Jesus' "rest" contrasts with the "heavy loads" Jesus' rival religious teachers laid on people's shoulders while "they themselves [were] not willing to lift a finger to move them" (Matt. 23:4). In the *New Interpreter's Bible* M. Eugene Boring comments, "Like 'rest,' the 'easy' yoke of Jesus is not an invitation to a life of ease, but of deliverance from the artificial burdens of human religion. . . . [Jesus' rest] is a synonym for salvation, associated with the kingdom of God and eternal life."

11:29—For the content of Jesus' "yoke" and for the teachings we "learn from" him, see the Sermon on the Mount (Matt. 5-7).

12:3-8—In *Matthew, a Commentary,* Frederick Dale Bruner notes that in the argument here Jesus refers to the Law and the Prophets, the temple, and the Sabbath—all of which are extremely important—and then claims to be "greater than the temple" and "Lord of the Sabbath." Bruner concludes, "The real theme of each controversy story is the *person* of Christ."

12:9—On the Sabbath, Jesus attends the "synagogue." Luke observes that attending synagogue "was his custom" (Luke 4:16). If we follow Jesus as disciples, we will "not give up meeting together, as some are in the habit of doing," but will "encourage one another—and all the more as [we] see the Day approaching" (Heb. 10:25).

12:14—The plot to "kill Jesus" is related not only to Jesus' Sabbath teachings and practice but also to the implicit claims Jesus makes about his authority. In another Sabbath-related passage we learn that in the eyes of Jesus' opponents, by healing and claiming authority to interpret the Sabbath as he does, and "even calling God his own Father," Jesus is "making himself equal with God" (John 5:18). In that same passage Jesus explains in some detail the relationship he has with the Father, making clear that his own work as the Son of God and Son of Man is to honor, depend on, and please the Father, who sent him (5:19-30).

GENERAL DISCUSSION

1. Are you a disciple of Jesus? Explain in terms of how this relates to Sabbath observance based on Jesus' teaching.

2. Are Sunday and the Sabbath the same thing? Explain.

3. According to Jesus, what is lawful on the Sabbath? (See Matt. 12:12.)

4. How long has it been since you have enjoyed a Sabbath?

SMALL GROUP SESSION IDEAS

Opening (10-15 minutes)

Pray/Worship—In your opening prayer for this session, take time to acknowledge the fatigue, frustrations, and burdens many people feel. Ask Jesus, by his Holy Spirit, to teach you to learn from him and to take on his yoke that fits.

For an opening hymn you could sing "Jesus Calls Us; O'er the Tumult," and for guidance in prayer from the psalms you could pray (or base your prayer on) Psalm 127.

Share—Catch up with each other on how things are going in general and in goalsetting you may have committed to. Are there any areas in which you may be trying to take on a yoke that doesn't fit?

Focus—Someone once passed along a question to me that would be good to consider during this session: *Am I letting Christ carry me, or am I trying to carry Christ?*

Growing (35-40 minutes)

Read (optional)—Perhaps someone could read the Matthew passage as a narrator and someone else could read the voice of Jesus.

Discuss—In addition to the General Discussion questions, you may wish to think about and respond to some of these process questions:

- Do other people actually pressure me, or is much of my pressure self-imposed by a desire to impress others?

- Am I a workaholic? Why is it respectable in many circles to sound as if we are workaholics?
- Do I really believe God cares for me? Do I trust Jesus enough to cast my burdens on him?
- What are some good things I like to do that I haven't done for a long time?
- Who is my boss? What difference does (or should) it make to think of Jesus as my boss?

Goalsetting (5 minutes)

A fitting goal for this session would be to commit to observing Sabbath in a way that exercises Christian freedom. Part of setting this goal may involve thinking about other spoken and unspoken goals in your life. You may need to ask yourself, *Am I often trying to add one more item to an already hectic schedule? Or am I listening to Jesus as the one thing needed and ordering my priorities in line with observing all of life as Sabbath?*

Closing (10-15 minutes)

Preparing for Prayer—Mention burdens you may be dealing with, as well as other concerns you may have. Think also of praises to bring before the Lord of the Sabbath, especially that we can rest in him. Then, before going into prayer, read Jesus' words in Matthew 11:28-30.

Prayer—You may wish to begin your closing prayer with a minute or so of silence so that everyone can have some private time with God. Everyone may join in with petitions and praises. If you didn't read Psalm 127 earlier, you could do that now. Or you could read Psalm 92. For a closing prayer song, you could sing "Lord, Speak to Me That I May Speak" or another hymn that combines prayer with rest and mission.

Why should we listen to our parents?

5

DEUTERONOMY 5:16; EPHESIANS 6:1-9

Our First Teachers

In a Nutshell

The fifth commandment calls us to honor our parents. The practice of honoring parents brings out the parental office of teacher. By learning to listen to our parents, imperfect as they are, we learn to listen to God, who chooses to teach us through them. This listening equips us to be receptive to the teaching and authority of others for the Lord's sake, and, in turn, to train and instruct others in the Lord.

Deuteronomy 5:16

16"Honor your father and your mother, as the LORD your God has commanded you, so that you may live long and that it may go well with you in the land the LORD your God is giving you."

Ephesians 6:1-9

1Children, obey your parents in the
Lord, for this is right. 2"Honor your father
and mother"—which is the first commandment with a promise—3"that it may
go well with you and that you may enjoy long life on the earth."
4Fathers, do not exasperate your children; instead, bring them up in the training and instruction of the Lord.
5Slaves, obey your earthly masters with respect and fear, and with sincerity of heart, just as you would obey Christ.
6Obey them not only to win their favor when their eye is on you, but like slaves of Christ, doing the will of God from your
heart. 7Serve wholeheartedly, as if you
were serving the Lord, not men, 8because
you know that the Lord will reward everyone for whatever good he does, whether he is slave or free.
9And masters, treat your slaves in the same way. Do not threaten them, since you know that he who is both their Master and yours is in heaven, and there is no favoritism with him.

The Home as "Shul" (Synagogue School)

In *The Color of Water: A Black Man's Tribute to His White Mother,* James McBride tells the remarkable story of his mother, Ruth. Ruth McBride Jordan raised twelve children and managed to send all of them to college. Twice a widow and never economically well-off, Mrs. McBride Jordan achieved this feat while staving off the pressures of poverty, racism, and criminal activity that threatened her home in Harlem. James McBride cites his mother's Jewishness as the reason for her dedication to education. Though she converted to Christianity as a young woman, one bit of heritage she retained from her Jewish childhood was the sense that raising children to do their best in school is a sacred obligation that God lays on parents.

Mrs. McBride Jordan's accomplishments shine even more brightly against the shadow of her personal background. Her own father never showed her affection. Instead, he mistreated everyone in the family, and he sexually abused Ruth during her girlhood. Mrs. McBride Jordan describes this abuse as a "nightmare." But when it came to providing for her education, she says of her father, "He wasn't cheap; I'll say that for him." In spite of his horrible failures in the most important personal aspects of fatherhood, Mr. Shilsky obeyed his calling to educate his children. And for that, Mrs. McBride Jordan, without denying the evil she suffered at her father's hands, was also able to honor him.

Ruth McBride Jordan's painful story brings out an aspect of parent-children relationships that is central to the Bible but is often forgotten in our day: *Parents are their children's first teachers.* All parents are imperfect teachers. Some of them are terrible teachers. In any case, we need to understand our parents and learn how we can rightly honor them. By learning to listen to them, we learn to listen to God.

Love Is Not All We Need

In Ephesians 6 Paul instructs his readers, "Children, obey your parents in the Lord, for this is right" (Eph. 6:1). Paul then quotes the fifth commandment, which says, "Honor your father and mother" (6:2; see Deut. 5:16).

In order to honor our parents, we need to see them as more than people who love us (or fail to love us). We need to see them as teachers. Teaching is, so to speak, a public office for parents. Paul makes this explicit when he goes on to say, "Fathers, do not exasperate your children; instead, bring them up in the training and instruction of the Lord" (Eph. 6:4).

In ancient societies, the father was generally seen as the authority figure over not only a nuclear family but also an extended household. This household could include several generations of relatives and, in some cases, servants or slaves. In such settings, fathers played many roles that we tend to compartmentalize today. As Lewis Smedes observes in his book *Mere Morality,* Hebrew children were accustomed to see their fathers "as clan ruler, warrior, high priest, and judge, as well as father." They would see their mothers in various roles as well (see, for example, Prov. 31). The children knew they had to learn these roles themselves, so it made sense to them to honor their parents as teachers.

Smedes notes further that children honored their parents throughout their lives. In childhood, this meant primarily listening and obeying in order to learn. Later in life this would often mean becoming their parents' caretakers. The important point to see is that for both young and adult children, honor is distinct from the warm feelings of love that all of us crave. Surveying biblical passages relating to the fifth commandment, Smedes notes, "What we distill is an unsentimental notion of honor, not the platitudes of the typical Mother's Day card, but moral commitment to filial respect and long-term loyalty."

Honor Authority

We obey and honor parents because, as the Heidelberg Catechism puts it, "through them God chooses to rule us" (Q&A 104). Even in the structure and wording of the Decalogue we can see the God-given importance of parents.

The Christian tradition has often spoken of the law as being divided into "two tables." Taking a cue from Jesus' summary of the law as *love of God* and *love of neighbor,* many Christians have seen the first four commandments—the first table of the law—as ordering our relationship to God and the final six commandments—the second table of the law—as ordering our relationships to our neighbors. (See, for example, Heidelberg Catechism, Q&A 93.)

One can also make a case, though, that the fifth commandment is closely related to the first table. In the first four commandments the name of "the LORD" is either explicitly stated or clearly implied (as in the first commandment, by the word "me"). In the last five commandments, the focus is on neighbors, and the name of "the LORD" is not mentioned. Yet in the fifth commandment we find the phrase "as the LORD your God has commanded you" (Deut. 5:16). The name of "the LORD" also occurs a second time in connection with the promise attached to this command, the promise highlighted by Paul in Ephesians 6:2.

So the fifth commandment, while moving us into the second table of the law to focus on neighbors, reveals how closely related are the practices of honoring our parents and honoring the Lord. In God's plan, the first people to represent God to us are our parents.

The structure and wording of the fifth commandment, as well as the vital importance of parents in our relationship with God, place an awesome obligation on parents. These same factors also place a compelling obligation on children. We often hear that we should "question authority." This can be a good thing, and at times it is necessary. Jesus himself calls us, for example, not only to question but even to reject any authority that conflicts with his (see Matt. 10:37-38; 23:9). But questioning authority becomes irresponsible if we divorce it from God's command to honor our fathers and mothers. For a society to live in the world God made, we need to honor not only our parents but also all the people God puts in authority over us.

Households as Missions

Studying the fifth commandment recalls many of the themes we discussed in our study of the first commandment as expressed positively in Deuteronomy 6:5-7. In God's plan, households can serve as mission stations, and parents are called to act as evangelists. In addition to teaching the gospel directly to their children and to other people in their household, good parents serve the cause of the gospel indirectly by providing a stable environment in which the gospel can be heard.

Some historians of missions attribute the growth of Christianity in the first three centuries A.D. primarily to Christian households, which were the foundation of household churches. (Note, for example, Paul's references to Priscilla and Aquila and "the church that meets in their house"—Rom. 16:3-5; 1 Cor. 16:19.) Households led by godly parents can play a vital role in missions today as well.

Additional Notes

Eph. 6:2—The "promise" here is not a guarantee that obedience to parents will bring earthly well-being. It's a description of God's usual way of working and of the general truth that honoring parents makes for social well-being.

6:4—Paul's exhortation to fathers to teach their children echoes similar exhortations in Proverbs that include both fathers and mothers (see, for example, Prov. 1:8; 6:20). Perhaps fathers need to be reminded of this sacred obligation more than mothers do.

In *The Message of Ephesians,* John Stott points out that in the context of the patriarchal structures of Roman society, in which the *paterfamilias* ("father of the extended household family") had virtually unlimited authority, Paul's direct address to children together with his restraint on fathers considerably modified the often harsh fatherly discipline of that day. Paul wanted fathers and mothers to reflect the Lord, who said, "Let the little children come to me," and who then took children in his arms and blessed them (Mark 10:14-16).

6:5—As the *NIV Study Bible* points out regarding "slaves," the Scriptures do not mandate slavery when they recognize its reality. Given the hardness of human hearts, evils such as slavery exist. The Scriptures point to godly ways to obey God in fallen conditions. Even when slavery is abolished, economic systems are still fallen, and we need wisdom on how to serve God faithfully in difficult settings.

6:9—Paul's declaration that the Lord is the Master of masters as well as of slaves plants seeds toward the growth of democratic human rights, as John Stott also notes in *The Message of Ephesians.*

GENERAL DISCUSSION

1. To what extent have you viewed your parents as teachers?

2. How do you respond to this explanation of the fifth commandment from the Heidelberg Catechism (Q&A 104): "that I obey and submit to [my father and mother and all those in authority over me], as is proper, when they correct and punish me; and also that I be patient with their failings—for through them God chooses to rule us"?

3. Suppose a high school student from a non-Christian home converts to Christ against the will of his or her parents. How can that teenager obey the fifth commandment?

4. How does the command to honor parents relate to Paul's further instructions to obey earthly masters?

SMALL GROUP SESSION IDEAS

Opening (10-15 minutes)

Pray/Worship—To open with a prayer focusing on themes in this session, you could pray with gratitude for parents and other authorities in our lives, asking for wisdom to discern how best to honor them in line with God's will for us.

It would also be fitting to read Psalm 119:33-40. The hymn "Tell Your Children" would also be appropriate either at this point or at the end of your session.

Share—Take some time to reflect on goals you have set as individuals or as a group. Have you taken a Sabbath recently? Has the Sabbath discussion from lesson 4 had any effect on your goalsetting?

Focus—Throughout this session consider how you can answer questions like these: *How did (or do) my parents reflect God's character? How did (or do) they not? How can I honor them, as well as the other authorities in my life?*

Growing (35-40 minutes)

Read (optional)—One way to read the Scripture passages for this session would be to have as many people as possible read, either by taking turns verse by verse, or (if you have a large group) reading in unison.

Discuss—In addition to the General Discussion questions, consider responding to some of the following:

- Who are the parent figures in your life? In what ways have they pointed you toward the Lord?
- Have you ever tried to put yourself in the shoes of politicians, principals, pastors, and others who must balance the interests of various groups of people? If so, how did that affect your perspective?
- If your parents are still alive, do you have a mature, adult-to-adult relationship with them? Explain.
- If you have children, do you listen to them? Explain.

Goalsetting (5 minutes)
Perhaps one goal you can set in response to this lesson is to express your thanks to a parent or some other parent figure or authority in your life. Consider doing so in a memorable personal way, either in writing or in conversation or perhaps with a gift included. Thank the Lord also for this person in your life, and live out your gratitude to God by honoring this person and showing others how to honor parents and other authority figures.

Closing (10-15 minutes)
Preparing for Prayer—Some of you may be processing deep feelings about parents or other authorities in your lives. While some may be feeling grateful and eager to express thanks, others may be struggling with issues of abandonment, poor role-modeling, and/or abuse. Be sensitive to whatever each other's experiences may have been, and look for ways to point each other to God as our loving, gracious parent who can be trusted to be "our refuge and strength" always (Ps. 46:1).

Prayer—You may wish to close this session with a "popcorn" prayer, in which anyone who wants to may offer a brief prayer at any time—even more than once, if desired. Periods of silence for private prayer may also be observed. When the person who opened the prayer senses it is time to close, he or she can do so.

You could also close this time of prayer by singing, "Lord, Listen to Your Children Praying."

Group Project (Optional)
In light of the Bible teachings about the obligations of government and other authorities, you and your group may be interested in a cause that works toward justice. As citizens of God's coming kingdom, we can live and work in hope toward the day when the kingdom comes in its fullness, when the Lord's rule of righteousness (justice) will restore the creation and bring an end to war, oppression, and all other suffering that afflicts people in this world. You'll want to check with health, welfare, political action, denominational, and environmental agencies for ideas and for help in getting started.

For example, you might help in a local immunization clinic, a blood drive, or a food program. Or you could help clean up a roadway, waterway, or disaster site. Or you could work toward human rights, legal justice, community safety, literacy and basic-skills education, biblical literacy, acceptance and education of mentally impaired persons, responsible medical research, preservation of wildlife, proper use of land, cleaner air and water—whatever you can think of. Every area of our lives and of this world is under Christ's authority, and he calls us to seek God's kingdom and righteousness even as we live in this world (Deut. 20:19-20; 22:6-7; Ps. 24:1-2; Matt. 6:33; Luke 12:31; Eph. 1:9-10; 4:1, 17-24; Rev. 22:1-2).

"Why are
you angry?"

6

DEUTERONOMY 5:17; MATTHEW 5:21-26

The Road to Hell

In a Nutshell

The sixth commandment prohibits murder. Jesus radicalizes this commandment to prohibit brooding anger, contempt, and all roots of murder. Although Jesus' teachings in this regard are hard to practice, the alternative—indulging anger in ways that lead to murderous hatred—is even harder. Positively, Jesus calls us to seek reconciliation. By practicing reconciliation, we imitate God in the promotion of life.

Deuteronomy 5:17

"You shall not murder."

Matthew 5:21-26

21"You have heard that it was said to
the people long ago, 'Do not murder, and
anyone who murders will be subject to
judgment.' 22But I tell you that anyone
who is angry with his brother will be subject to judgment. Again, anyone who says
to his brother, 'Raca,' is answerable to the Sanhedrin. But anyone who says, 'You fool!' will be in danger of the fire of hell.
23"Therefore, if you are offering your
gift at the altar and there remember that
your brother has something against you,
24leave your gift there in front of the altar.
First go and be reconciled to your brother; then come and offer your gift.
25"Settle matters quickly with your
adversary who is taking you to court. Do it while you are still with him on the way, or he may hand you over to the judge, and the judge may hand you over to the officer, and you may be thrown into prison.
26I tell you the truth, you will not get out
until you have paid the last penny."

"Ugh" Again?

In Lesson 3 we reflected on a story from Leviticus that strikes many people as harsh, and we wondered if it could make some people say, "Ugh." In this lesson, we encounter a passage that may strike us as harsh in a different way. On the one hand, Jesus' prohibition not only of murder but also of murderous emotions amazes us as a highly refined moral teaching. On the other hand, it may also strike us as impossible and, therefore, cruel. Who has not felt anger toward a brother or sister? Who has not called people names? Is Jesus inhumane to prohibit feelings and actions that it seems we can hardly avoid? It's possible to read this passage in a way that makes us feel hopelessly condemned by Jesus.

Reflex and Reflection

One helpful way out of that sort of interpretation is to note the Greek word Matthew uses to convey Jesus' teaching. Frederick Dale Bruner, following the lead of British scholar William Barclay, notes in *Matthew, a Commentary,* that there are "two main Greek words for anger." One word refers to a spark of anger that dies away as quickly as it leaps. That's not the word Matthew uses in this passage. The word Matthew uses (*orgizo*) refers to a lasting anger that someone harbors and nurtures. Unlike a spark that fades quickly, this kind of anger is like a fire that is carefully kindled, fed, and tended to keep it burning. In this passage, Jesus prohibits "long-lived anger . . . the anger of the man who nurses his wrath to keep it warm," states Barclay.

In light of this grammatical distinction, we can follow Bruner's translation of Matthew 5:22, which says, "Everyone who nurses a grudge against his brother will have to face the judgment." Jesus, then, does not condemn our built-in reflex to feel anger any more than he condemns our built-in reflex to feel pain. As Dallas Willard notes in a helpful discussion of this matter in *The Divine Conspiracy,* anger as "a spontaneous response . . . has a vital function in life. As such it is not wrong." But the sad reality is that spontaneous anger almost always turns into something evil because it inevitably contains some degree of malice. Jesus judges malicious anger and warns against where it can lead: to "the fire of hell" (Matt. 5:22).

The story of Cain helps us put flesh and blood on this warning. When the Lord did not look with favor on Cain and his offering, "Cain was very angry, and his face was downcast" (Gen. 4:5). God did not condemn Cain for his anger, but God did warn against the power of sin to use Cain's anger to destroy him. The Lord said, "Sin is crouching at your door; it desires to have you, but you must master it" (4:7). Cain failed to heed God's warning, and the consequences were deadly. Nursing a grudge, he murdered his brother and faced a life, in his own words, "hidden from [the Lord's] presence" (4:14). That's where anger threatens to lead us—away from the presence of the Lord.

One way to "master" the reflex of sinful anger is to reflect on the Lord's pastoral question to Cain: "Why are you angry?"

(4:6). When we pose that question honestly to ourselves, we discover that our "righteous" anger often is, at best, only partly justified. Almost always, our anger flows not only from having suffered some injustice but also from some insult to our inflated ego. Further, though we hesitate to acknowledge it, our anger is often directed ultimately against God. Whether we admit it or not, when we feel slighted, we often feel God has not shown us the favor we deserve, and we take out our anger against God by lashing out against brothers and sisters.

In this regard, it's revealing to notice that Cain's anger began in a worship setting of offering a sacrifice to God (4:3-5). Jesus too speaks of anger in the context of his followers' offering gifts "at the altar" (Matt. 5:23). This connection reminds us that our relationship with God is inextricably bound up with our relationships with our brothers and sisters. As 1 John 4:20-21 teaches, "If anyone says, 'I love God,' yet hates his brother, he is a liar. For anyone who does not love his brother, whom he has seen, cannot love God, whom he has not seen. And he has given us this command: Whoever loves God must also love his brother."

The Excellent Way

Graciously, Jesus holds out an alternative to the self-destructive way of anger. "First," he says, "go and be reconciled to your brother, then come and offer your gift" (Matt. 5:24). Striking the realistic note that permeates the Sermon on the Mount, Jesus illustrates reconciliation by advising us, "Settle matters quickly with your adversary who is taking you to court" (5:25). In the all-too-familiar settings of sibling rivalries, religious competition, and adversarial legal actions, Jesus urges the swift settlement of disputes. To practice this teaching, we will often need to swallow our pride, ask for forgiveness, and exercise forgiveness ourselves. In other words, we will need to imitate God, who humbly forgives us day after day.

Imitating God by means of forgiveness and love for enemies is hard. But the alternative is harder. Who of us wants to live locked up either in our own anger or in some actual prison where our anger could lead us? Jesus does not want us to languish in prisons of any kind. So he warns us graciously and realistically, "I tell you the truth, you will not get out until you have paid the last penny" (5:26).

Saying "Ugh" to the results of anger can motivate us to follow the "most excellent way" of love (1 Cor. 12:30-13:13).

Win-Win

Mastering anger and practicing reconciliation are essential to the mission of the church. For example, note how anger and evangelism contradict each other. But when we overcome anger with a genuine desire for the good of the people around us, we will inevitably want them to share our faith in Jesus. Paul expresses the connection between reconciliation and mission this way: God "has committed to us the message of reconciliation. We are therefore Christ's ambassadors, as though God were making his appeal through us. We implore you on Christ's behalf: Be reconciled to God" (2 Cor. 5:19-20). As we members of the church become reconciled to God, we will practice reconciliation among ourselves and toward unbelievers. In this way, we will win others to Christ.

Additional Notes

Matt. 5:21-22—Throughout the Sermon on the Mount, Jesus does not abolish but instead fulfills Old Testament instructions (see 5:17), which we can summarize as *torah* (see the section "Law as *Torah*" in lesson 1 of this leader's guide). When Jesus says, "You have heard . . . but I tell you . . ." he does not repudiate the Old Testament law. Nor does he contrast his message of love with a supposed message of wrath. Instead, Jesus *interprets* the *torah* for his disciples. He gets at the root meaning and intention of the commandments. (See also comments about the *lex talionis* in "Additional Notes" on Lev. 24:20 in lesson 3. This "law of retaliation," like related laws about cities of refuge—see Num. 35:6-34; Deut. 4:41-43—promotes proportional punishment on the part of authorized parties. When Jesus radicalizes these laws along with the sixth commandment, he is simply building on the path toward justice, reconciliation, and peace. And all the while he is following the Old Testament law of love as found in Lev. 19:18.)

The prohibition of murder refers to homicide. The Scriptures do not prohibit all killing.

The word "brother" indicates Jesus' emphasis that his disciples "love one another" (John 13:34). This love command applies to our brothers and sisters in the Christian church and to others as well, as other statements in the Sermon on the Mount indicate—such as Jesus' references to letting our light shine before others and loving our enemies because God loves everyone (see Matt. 5:13-16, 38-48). In John 13:35 Jesus further illustrates the missionary impetus of love among brothers and sisters by saying, "By this all men will know that you are my disciples, if you love one another."

The "judgment" here and throughout this passage seems to refer to the judgment of the covenant community as appointed by God. Compare Jesus' teaching in Matthew 18. There he instructs disciples to counsel one another regarding their faults. If two individuals cannot agree, first two or three witnesses and then the entire church should become involved. (Note also that the reference to the Sanhedrin in Matthew 5:22 points to a higher court of judgment that has more than local authority.) Then Jesus makes this sobering statement: "Whatever you bind on earth will be bound in heaven, and whatever you loose on earth will be loosed in heaven" (18:18). Jesus and his Father in heaven have chosen to exercise judgment and make their will known through the community of disciples. This awesome responsibility requires that we pray fervently for the Spirit of Christ to guide our understanding.

"Raca" means something like "empty-headed" or "airhead." It expresses contempt that flows from anger and can lead to murderous hatred.

As described in the Scriptures, a "fool" lacks more than intellectual ability. Folly flows from a disobedient rejection of God and God's ways (see Ps. 14:1). We'll discuss this matter in more detail in lesson 7, which deals with biblical wisdom in the context of moral living.

Biblical teachings on the "fire of hell" developed over time. In Matthew's Greek presentation of Jesus' teaching, Jesus refers to "Gehenna," a valley outside Jerusalem where trash was burned and where, historically, the Lord's people practiced pagan abominations such as human sacrifice. As the *NIV Study Bible* notes, this valley "became a sort of perpetually burning city dump and later a figure for the place of final punishment." (See 2 Kings 23:8-10; Jer. 7:30-33.)

5:23-26—Jesus' references to "the altar" and "court" do not offer an exhaustive interpretation of his teachings on murder and anger. Rather, they offer two common illustrations of situations in which we are tempted to nurture murderous hatred. By presenting these two provocative examples, Jesus points us to "the kind of righteousness appropriate to the kingdom of God," says M. Eugene Boring in *The New Interpreter's Bible.* Boring goes on to observe, "Disciples are responsible for using this example creatively to apply Jesus' teachings to their own situations."

GENERAL DISCUSSION

1. Is it easy to agree with the connection Jesus makes between murder and anger? How does Jesus' teaching on anger make you feel?

2. How would you explain to a skeptical friend why Jesus sees such a close connection between anger and murder?

3. Read again Jesus' words in Matthew 5:23-24 about offering a gift "at the altar." How would you restate those words in more contemporary terms or try to explain them with a contemporary illustration?

4. List some contemporary issues to which the sixth commandment speaks most directly. How does Jesus' teaching on anger guide us in dealing with these issues?

SMALL GROUP SESSION IDEAS

Opening (10-15 minutes)

Pray/Worship—In your opening prayer for this session you may wish to pick up on the structure and content of the Sermon on the Mount. In other words, you could begin with praise and thanks to God for blessing those who are poor in spirit by welcoming them into the kingdom of heaven. Then you could confess to falling short of our Lord's calling to love and forgive. You could also ask the Spirit to inspire each of you to follow the narrow way that leads to life. Pray, as well, for wisdom to put Christ's teachings into practice as you study the Bible together and as you go about your daily living.

If you'd like to include music, you could also sing together "Make Me a Channel of Your Peace"—either now or at the end of this session.

Share—Take a little time to catch up with each other and to see how you're doing on goals you've set or on matters raised by the material for this session.

Focus—Throughout this session, one way to focus on the main topic would be to ask yourself the question God asked Cain: *"Why are you angry?"* (Gen. 4:6). Or perhaps you could ask the Holy Spirit to help you see (or keep learning) ways in which you can improve on dealing with anger.

Growing (35-40 minutes)

Read (optional)—Since the Bible passages for this session are quite short, you may wish to read some other related sections of the Sermon on the Mount, such as Matthew 5:38-48 and 7:1-5.

Discuss—In addition to the General Discussion questions, you may wish to ask yourself and perhaps discuss the following questions wherever they best fit:

- Do people see me as a generally angry person?
- Do I have a lot of anger that people do not see?
- Have I ever wondered whether I should not participate in the Lord's Supper because of some personal conflict?
- Am I honest about my feelings? Are there people I hate or struggle not to hate?
- Does Jesus' teaching in this passage frighten me?

Goalsetting (5 minutes)

Perhaps you could try to offer (and perhaps even write down) prayers of confession about anger, contempt, or hatred that you might feel toward people. Such prayers make for the "most excellent" way to begin the process of forgiveness and reconciliation in Christ.

Closing (10-15 minutes)

Preparing for Prayer—Consider reading Luke 6:27-38. Observe together how Jesus calls us to show love, mercy, and forgiveness when we are in situations in which we can easily be tempted to hateful anger. If you have time, think of some situations in your everyday life in which you could be tempted to react hatefully, and then think of ways to respond in line with Jesus' teaching.

Take time also to mention prayer concerns and praises, including items that may have come up during this session.

Prayer—After some opening words of prayer, move into a time of silent prayer and confession. Close by saying the Lord's Prayer in unison.

Group Study Project (Optional)

Lewis Smedes has written two helpful books on forgiveness: *Forgive and Forget: Healing the Hurts We Don't Deserve* (San Francisco: Harper & Row, 1984) and *The Art of Forgiving: When You Need to Forgive and Don't Know How* (Nashville: Moorings, 1996). Some of you may wish to read and report on one of these during a later session of this study.

Group Project (Optional)

If you're interested in pursuing justice issues by positively applying the sixth commandment in our world today, see ideas listed in the group project suggestion at the end of lesson 5.

Why get married?

7

DEUTERONOMY 5:18; PROVERBS 5

The Ways of Life and Death

In a Nutshell

The seventh commandment prohibits adultery and, by extension, all sexual immorality. Positively, it calls us to express our sexuality in covenantal ways. Proverbs 5 portrays both the deadly folly of adultery and the joyful wisdom of marriage. Thinking about sex in terms of biblical wisdom helps us avoid disaster and celebrate marriage.

Deuteronomy 5:18

"You shall not commit adultery."

Proverbs 5

1My son, pay attention to my wisdom,
listen well to my words of insight,
2that you may maintain discretion
and your lips may preserve
knowledge.
3For the lips of an adulteress drip honey,
and her speech is smoother than oil;
4but in the end she is bitter as gall,
sharp as a double-edged sword.
5Her feet go down to death;
her steps lead straight to the grave.
6She gives no thought to the way of life;
her paths are crooked, but she
knows it not.

7Now then, my sons, listen to me;
do not turn aside from what I say.
8Keep to a path far from her,
do not go near the door of her house,
9lest you give your best strength to others
and your years to one who is cruel,
10lest strangers feast on your wealth
and your toil enrich another man's
house.
11At the end of your life you will groan,
when your flesh and body are spent.
12You will say, "How I hated discipline!
How my heart spurned correction!
13I would not obey my teachers
or listen to my instructors.
14I have come to the brink of utter ruin
in the midst of the whole assembly."

15Drink water from your own cistern,
running water from your own well.
16Should your springs overflow in
the streets,
your streams of water in the public
squares?
17Let them be yours alone,
never to be shared with strangers.
18May your fountain be blessed,
and may you rejoice in the wife of
your youth.
19A loving doe, a graceful deer—
may her breasts satisfy you always,
may you ever be captivated by her love.

20Why be captivated, my son, by an
adulteress?
Why embrace the bosom of another
man's wife?
21For a man's ways are in full view of
the LORD,
and he examines all his paths.
22The evil deeds of a wicked man
ensnare him;
the cords of his sin hold him fast.
23He will die for lack of discipline,
led astray by his own great folly.

A Common but True Tale

More than once I have witnessed a story that follows this pattern: A young man and woman find each other attractive and sleep together, and the young woman becomes pregnant. Though they have not obeyed Christian teachings about premarital sex, both partners are from Christian homes and are Christians themselves. They do not seriously consider abortion. Instead, they decide marriage is the right thing to do. Not knowing each other very well and experiencing the added pressure of childcare, their marriage gets off to a rocky start. In some cases they stay married; in others, they divorce. Either way, they experience hardship beyond what they ever imagined on the night their child was conceived.

Sexual Immorality Is Stupid

In Proverbs 5 a wise teacher gives a no-nonsense lesson about sexual immorality. The teacher warns against sexual relationships that taste sweet to begin with but, in the end, are "bitter as gall" (Prov. 5:4). Proverbs 5 addresses young men and warns against "an adulteress" (or "loose woman," RSV). But the lesson applies to young and old, and to men and women alike. If a person wanders outside the bounds of God's instructions on sexuality, that person walks toward death.

The wisdom teacher in Proverbs points out that sexual immorality leads not only to a bad end but also to hardship along the way. For example, the effort involved in adultery makes a person vulnerable to cruelty, thievery, and even to betrayal (5:9-10). Sexual immorality is dangerous to body and soul (5:11-13). It can lead to public humiliation "in the midst of the whole assembly" (5:14). Such sin is also "in full view of the LORD" (5:21), and the wages are finally death (5:23). Those who listen to the teacher and shudder at the possibilities described here can avoid the remorseful groans the adulterer laments in this passage: "How I hated discipline! How my heart spurned correction!" (5:12).

Wisely, the teacher also does more than portray the negative consequences of sexual immorality. Proverbs 5 also describes the joys of sex within the bounds of marriage. With words that, in the context of a Bible study at least, may make us blush, the teacher holds out this intoxicating invitation: "A loving doe, a graceful deer—may her breasts satisfy you always, may you ever be captivated by her love" (5:19). The biblical sexual ethic is not only uncompromising but also life-affirming. This and many other biblical passages about marriage breathe the joyful spirit of the creation account, where our good God says, "Be fruitful and increase in number" (Gen. 1:28). Human sexuality is a good gift from the Creator.

Mature believers, then, can pass this message along to promote joy, especially among the young. God gives us a glad alternative to sexual immorality; God gives us marriage in which to enjoy the good gift of moral sexuality.

Marriage Is Wise

The Bible teaches not only the joy of sex within marriage but also the wisdom of marriage. Proverbs especially is known as a wisdom book, and it's part of a tradition of wisdom literature. Wisdom helps us live well by teaching us to understand reality. When we live in harmony with reality, we improve our possibilities of enjoying happiness and success. We go wrong, of course, if we seek happiness directly or at the expense of obedience. And we commit heresy if we confuse success with salvation. But it's right to recognize that obedience in the form of godly wisdom often leads to happiness and success.

Wisdom illumines every realm of life in God's good creation, but today one area in which we need lots of wisdom is the realm of sexuality. With respect to sex, even otherwise sensible and highly moral people often make stupid mistakes. One reason for this is the false advertising—the denial of reality—that has accompanied the sexual revolution of the past several decades. The so-called liberation of sex from traditional restraints has not brought about sexual happiness. Instead, it has helped to promote misery in the form of false expectations, broken marriages, pornography, sexual addictions, sexual abuse, sexually transmitted diseases, and more.

To say this is not to romanticize past eras in which phrases like "fallen from grace" or "loss of virtue" tended to equate grace and virtue with sexual respectability. Nor is it to promote prudery or any other distorted view of sex. It's simply to encourage realistic, biblical thinking about sex. Sex is important, and, in the setting of marriage, sexual intercourse is a blessing.

The converse of this teaching is that obsessive and even idolatrous views of sex are a curse.

In the language of Proverbs, sexual immorality is folly, and sexual obedience is wise. Let's encourage one another to live wisely in the realm of sexuality. Let's encourage one another to choose obedience and, therefore, to "choose life" (Deut. 30:19).

Marriage and Mission

One of the most effective evangelism programs to emerge in recent times is an inquirer-oriented introduction to the Christian faith called "The Alpha Course." From small beginnings in an Anglican Church in London, England, Alpha programs have spread all over the world. What's more, some Alpha organizers plan to follow up this evangelistic course with a course designed to encourage and strengthen marriages. They have seen what should be clear to us all. Human sexuality and marriage are so important in human community that a divine word of wisdom on these topics brings life and hope to all who have ears to hear. Believers who promote God's wisdom in sexuality serve the mission of God on earth by bringing good news for everyday living.

Additional Notes

Prov. 5:1—Proverbs depicts a teacher addressing someone whom he calls "my son." With careful and creative listening, we can certainly hear the wisdom teacher addressing daughters as well as sons. Proverbs expresses God's word to all people.

5:3—The Hebrew term translated here as "adulteress" or "loose woman" can be translated more literally as "strange woman," "foreign woman," or "alien woman" (see also 2:16-17). The idea is that this woman is out of bounds. She is not inherently evil. In fact, like human sexuality itself, she is a good creature of God. But sexual union with her outside the bounds of marriage is disobedience.

5:6—The term "way of life" is common in wisdom literature. It refers to a lifelong following of God's instructions as the best way to live. Psalm 1, a wisdom psalm, contrasts "the way of the righteous" with "the way of the wicked" (Ps. 1:6). In wisdom writings, wisdom and righteousness are closely related. Proverbs 5 also includes other images related to "the way of life"—for example, see "steps" and "paths" in 5:5-6.

5:11—The groans associated with "flesh and body" here could refer to sexually transmitted diseases or other physical disabilities related to immorality. They could also be regrets over broken relationships that linger into old age. As in other wisdom passages, the reference seems deliberately open-ended, suggesting various unpleasant possibilities. Such "open-endedness permits the reader to apply the admonition to his or her own life-world, whatever the circumstances may be," writes Raymond Van Leeuwen in his commentary on Proverbs in *The New Interpreter's Bible.*

5:15-19—In these verses, various water images refer to a loving marital relationship. Van Leeuwen points out that in arid Palestine, water is exceedingly precious. Note that the descriptions of water sources in this passage grow progressively more precious or personally valued.

GENERAL DISCUSSION

1. Do the wisdom teachings about sex and marriage in Proverbs 5 agree with your experience and observations?

2. Read John 7:53-8:11. What does Jesus say to the woman caught in adultery? In what ways does this passage help to balance or expand on the message of Proverbs 5?

3. Why do many people today fear and avoid marriage?

4. Reflect on the wisdom teacher's call to discipline in sexuality, marriage, and all of life.

SMALL GROUP SESSION IDEAS

Opening (10-15 minutes)

Pray/Worship—In your opening prayer, ask the Holy Spirit to guide your group to discuss sexuality both honestly and appropriately. Pray also for wisdom.

If you like joining together in song, you could sing the hymn "Praised Be the Father" either at the beginning or at the end of this session.

Share—Spend some time catching up with each other and discussing your goalsetting or other features of this Bible study.

Focus—Throughout this session, consider the following question: *Have I prayed faithfully for God's wisdom with regard to my sexuality?*

Growing (35-40 minutes)

Read (optional)—Either one reader or several can read the passages for this session, or you could read them in unison.

Discuss—In addition to the General Discussion questions, reflect on and consider discussing the following process questions wherever they may fit:

- Did my parents or anyone else ever give me straightforward biblical teachings about sexuality?
- In what circumstances am I most vulnerable to sexual temptation? How can spiritual disciplines help me in this area?
- In the most important relationships and friendships we have, what can we do keep them alive and healthy?
- Do I pray for the fruit of the Spirit as found in Galatians 5:22-23? What does "self-control" mean to me?

Goalsetting (5 minutes)

A fitting goal as a result of this session would be to work at renewing relationships. Friends and singles can think of creative ways to spend good times together. Married couples can think of ways to enjoy each other's company and keep their romance alive.

Closing (10-15 minutes)

Preparing for Prayer—To build on the closing part of your discussion, you could prepare for prayer by reading the fruit of the Spirit passage in Galatians 5:22-23 and then shape your prayer in terms of the fruit mentioned there. Be sure also to mention praises and concerns that you'd like the group to pray about.

Prayer—Offer thanks to our great God for good friends, companions, marriage, and sexuality. Pray about each other's praises and concerns—either silently or out loud. Pray also for the Holy Spirit to guide you in wisdom each day.

8

DEUTERONOMY 5:19; EPHESIANS 4:22-5:2

Imitators of God

In a Nutshell

The eighth commandment forbids stealing. By extension, it forbids any form of cheating our neighbor and any form of idolatrous greed. Positively, the eighth commandment calls us to love our neighbor in the form of producing goods and sharing them. As our passage from Ephesians indicates, the positive obedience of work expresses our identity as new creatures in Christ. When we work in order to share, we imitate God as revealed in Christ, and we offer up a "fragrant offering and sacrifice to God" (Eph. 5:2).

Deuteronomy 5:19

"You shall not steal."

Ephesians 4:22-32

[22]You were taught, with regard to your former way of life, to put off your old self, which is being corrupted by its deceitful desires; [23]to be made new in the attitude of your minds; [24]and to put on the new self, created to be like God in true righteousness and holiness.

[25]Therefore each of you must put off falsehood and speak truthfully to his neighbor, for we are all members of one body. [26]"In your anger do not sin": Do not let the sun go down while you are still angry, [27]and do not give the devil a foothold. [28]He who has been stealing must steal no longer, but must work, doing something useful with his own hands, that he may have something to share with those in need.

[29]Do not let any unwholesome talk come out of your mouths, but only what is helpful for building others up according to their needs, that it may benefit those who listen. [30]And do not grieve the Holy Spirit of God, with whom you were sealed for the day of redemption. [31]Get rid of all bitterness, rage and anger, brawling and slander, along with every form of malice. [32]Be kind and compassionate to one another, forgiving each other, just as in Christ God forgave you.

5:1-2

[1]Be imitators of God, therefore, as dearly loved children [2]and live a life of love, just as Christ loved us and gave himself up for us as a fragrant offering and sacrifice to God.

Our Possessions and Our Selves

It's not uncommon for people who have been robbed to feel personally violated. This feeling makes sense because we have a personal relationship to our possessions. The money in my wallet is something I earned in a specific way. The tape player in my car has given me important memories and made long trips into pleasant excursions. The house where I live is a place where I want my family to feel safe. If someone steals my wallet, rips off my tape player, or breaks into my house, I lose more than money or a material possession. I lose time and effort. I lose something that matters to me, and I lose a feeling of security. People who have been robbed can suffer nightmares or other serious effects of trauma.

People who have been robbed can also gain a greater understanding of people whose wallets are always empty, who don't even own tape players or cars, and who might not even have a place to live. We see this happen, for example, in the Shakespearean character King Lear. Having been robbed of his possessions and of all dignity by two of his daughters, Lear eventually feels convicted of his own neglect of the poor. He offers a prayer of sorts for the poor that includes the confession: "O, I have ta'en too little care of this!" (Act III, Scene IV). Perhaps by reflecting on the eighth commandment we can gain a greater sense of care for people who live as our Lord once did, having "no place to lay [their heads]" (Luke 9:58).

Work So That

In our passage from Ephesians for this lesson we find only a few words directly related to stealing. "He who has been stealing must steal no longer," says Paul (Eph. 4:28).

This simple restatement of the eighth commandment may seem hardly relevant to Christians who never engage in outright acts of theft, such as shoplifting or armed robbery. But now that we've studied several of the Ten Commandments, we're learning that each of them tends to have rather comprehensive applications for us all.

In his book *Do We Still Need the Ten Commandments?* for example, John H. Timmerman recalls a time when he committed to support a younger member of his church by praying for him regularly. Over time, however, Timmerman's attention to this commitment lapsed, and, he writes, "By the end of the year, I thought of my partner's name with more guilt than support." Timmerman makes a good case that this broken commitment was a form of stealing—namely, a theft of trust.

Once we begin thinking along these lines, we can see, as Timmerman argues, that the eighth commandment reaches not only into the realm of commitments but also into such areas as "sins of commission and omission, our use of God-given gifts, and our stewardship of God's creation." As we recognize that we all fall short in all of these areas, we can see that Timmerman is thinking in a biblical way about theft and giving. Ephesians 4:25-5:2 gives us a view into that way of thinking.

Paul's command to stop stealing comes in the context of a comprehensive description of the Christian life. Paul has been urging the Ephesians to live up to their new identity as new creatures in Jesus Christ (Eph. 4:22-24). Being re-created by God, each believer "must put off falsehood and speak truthfully to his neighbor," says Paul, "for we are all members of one body" (4:25). Honest speech reflects our new identity in Christ, and it fits the new humanity of which we are a part.

The same considerations apply to honest work and to its opposite. Stealing is not an isolated act. Stealing denies our status in Christ and violates our neighbors. Honest work, on the other hand, expresses our identity in Christ and makes it possible for us to "share with those in need" (4:28). When we work, we imitate God our Creator, who made us in his image so that we could take care of the earth by ruling over it, caring for it, and doing good work in it (Gen. 1-2). And when we work in order to give, we imitate not only God who gave us Christ, but also Christ himself, who "gave himself up for us" (Eph. 5:1-2). The opposite of stealing is honest work that makes giving possible. When we work in order to give, we become, like Christ, "a fragrant offering and sacrifice to God" (5:2).

Work and Giving

Paul's references to our new creation in Christ suggest that we need to understand these teachings about stealing and work in light of God's initial creation of humanity. In Genesis 1 we learn that humanity is created in God's image and that we reflect God to our fellow creatures by taking care of them: "God said, 'Let us make man in our image, in our likeness, and let them rule over the fish of the sea and . . . [the other creatures of] the earth'" (Gen. 1:26). We can call this rule over all other creatures dominion or stewardship, and, in either case, we can realize that one major expression of stewardship happens in our daily work. God placed Adam "in the Garden of Eden to work it and take care of it" (2:15).

When we work and take care of our fellow creatures, we image God; we do what God created us to do. This is the connection between Paul's two statements in our passage: (1) "He who has been stealing must steal no longer, but must work, doing something useful with his own hands, that he may have something to share with those in need" (Eph. 4:28) and (2) "Be imitators of God" (5:1).

Again, when we work, we imitate God our Creator. And when we work in order to share, we imitate God our Redeemer. Work is an important realm in which we can "live a life of love, just as Christ loved us and gave himself up for us" (5:2). So let's give of ourselves by working for others to the glory of God and, in this way, offer "a fragrant offering and sacrifice to God" (5:2).

Work and Mission

Work relates to God's mission on earth in several ways. First, the people we work with are people we can share the good news of Jesus with. We cannot force this witness, of course, and common sense tells us not to come on too strong evangelistically in some workplaces. But if we pray to the Lord of the harvest for opportunities to work in his harvest wherever we do our work—whether it's in a factory, a corporate office, at home, on the road, in the marketplace, or elsewhere—we can trust that God will hear our prayer (see Matt. 9:35-38). We can pray and stay alert for opportunities to teach Christ in winning ways while we work.

Also, our work itself is part of our Lord's mission to reclaim creation as God's kingdom of peace. Competence and courtesy in our work can give people a taste of what God wanted for human workers in the Garden of Eden. Diligent service to Christ in all our work can be a foretaste of our stewardship over the new creation. And good work, in this time between the creation and the new creation, can become a way for us to bless many people—as in the way Joseph blessed Potiphar, his own family, and finally all the nations known to him during a time of great famine. By working as a manager in Egypt, and even as a prisoner for a crime he didn't commit, Joseph carried on God's mission to bless God's creation. As Joseph himself said, "It was to save lives that God sent me [to Egypt]" (Gen. 45:5).

May we see our work and our giving as ways God intends for us to be involved in the saving of many lives. May we see work as a setting in which we can obey Jesus' commandment "Be merciful, just as your Father is merciful" (Luke 6:36).

Additional Notes

Eph. 4:22-24—When Paul urges his readers to "put off the old self," he's referring to the old human nature we have inherited from fallen Adam. The positive counterpart to this putting off is the putting on of "the new self," the new humanity we receive from Christ. When we put on this "Christ humanity," we tell the truth, work, share, and live a life patterned after Christ's love.

4:27—Paul expounds on his reference to "the devil" later in Ephesians in the well-known "armor of God" passage (6:10-18). For Paul, all creation is a battleground between the true King, Christ, and the rebel king, Satan. We fight for Christ and against Satan in such everyday ways as making up with each other at home, doing our best at work, and living as our Creator intends (in other words, following "the way of life" we discussed in lesson 7).

4:28—The words "he who has been stealing" may well point to an ex-thief in Ephesus whose recovery is still in progress. Paul exhorts believers to honest work also in 1 Thessalonians 4. Apparently some believers had become busybodies and had been thinking and talking too much about Jesus' second coming. Paul tells them to get to work. Paul himself worked with his own hands (see 1 Cor. 4:12), and he did not want believers to misunderstand spirituality in a way that led them to neglect or defame honest labor. Respect for work fits the creation-to-new-creation drama of the Bible.

5:1—Regarding Paul's instruction "Be imitators of God," John Stott observes in *The Message of Ephesians,* "It is noteworthy how God-centered Paul's ethic is. It is natural for him, in issuing his moral instructions, to mention the three Persons of the Trinity. He tells us to 'copy God,' to 'learn Christ,' and not to 'grieve the Holy Spirit.'"

5:2—"live a life of love." A more direct translation of this verse renders Paul urging us to "walk in love." The notion of the Christian life as a "walk" in the way of obedience is a rich biblical image. See Psalm 1 and many passages in Proverbs about walking in the wise way of righteousness as opposed to the foolish way of disobedience, as we discussed in lesson 7. Jesus also uses this biblical image in his Sermon on the Mount (see Matt. 7:13-14).

GENERAL DISCUSSION

1. How does Paul's reference to the eighth commandment fit in with the "big idea" of conversion in Ephesians 4-5?

2. Do you think John H. Timmerman is too hard on himself when he sees his failure to pray for someone as a theft of trust? Explain.

3. How do you feel about your job?

4. How does your work fit in with God's mission?

SMALL GROUP SESSION IDEAS

Opening (10-15 minutes)

You may wish to begin this session with a reading from Genesis 1, Psalm 8, or Psalm 104. In the context of seeing the Creator at work in creation, you could think about how each one of us "goes out to . . . work" or how we labor in one way or another "until evening" (Ps. 104:23). This picture presents a highly positive alternative to stealing.

Pray/Worship—If your group likes to sing, you might try "Earth and All Stars," "For the Beauty of the Earth," or any other hymn about creation. In your opening prayer, you could give thanks for everyone's gifts and abilities and ask the Spirit to move you more and more toward perfect generosity.

Share—Take some time to update one another on how you're doing on goals you've set and in other areas of your lives.

Focus—Throughout this session keep in mind the question *Why did God give me the abilities I have?*

Growing (35-40 minutes)

Read (optional)—Read the passages for this session together as a group, if you like, before moving into your discussion time.

Discuss—In addition to the General Discussion questions, consider responding to the following as a way to process and apply the lesson material more personally:

- Have I ever been robbed or known someone who has been robbed? How does it feel to be robbed?
- Have I ever stolen something—not only in the broader sense of stealing someone's trust, but also in the sense of taking something that did not belong to me? If so, why did I do that?
- What are specific ways I can "put off" my "Adam self"? What are specific ways I can "put on" my "Christ self"?
- What are ways in which I share with others? Are there some ways in which I could expand my generosity?

Goalsetting (5 minutes)

Think of a particular person or good cause that needs help—financial or otherwise. Set a goal of sharing in a specific way. You can do this individually or as a group.

Closing (10-15 minutes)

Preparing for Prayer—Spend some time counting your blessings—both privately and together with group members. Consider God's generosity and some ways in which you can imitate it. Be sure also to mention concerns, including items or issues that have come up during this session.

Pray—As you pray together, ask the Holy Spirit to give all of you the gift of generosity. Pray for a spirit of cheerful and loving giving. Thank God for all the blessings you enjoy, ask for help or strength where it's needed, and praise God for answered prayers and for the biblical vision of serving the Lord with gladness in all you do.

Group Project (Optional)

For activities that can help you get into living and working in the hope of God's kingdom, see ideas listed in the group project suggestion at the end of lesson 5.

Why tell the truth?

9

DEUTERONOMY 5:20; 1 KINGS 21:1-16

A Tangled Web

In a Nutshell

The ninth commandment prohibits false testimony against our neighbors in a court of law. It doesn't absolutely forbid the use of deception in all circumstances, but it does issue a strong calling to tell the truth for the sake of our neighbors. The story of Naboth's vineyard illustrates the deadly effects of false witness. It also implies the importance of truth telling in the fight for God's kingdom against the kingdom of Satan.

Deuteronomy 5:20

"You shall not give false testimony against your neighbor."

1 Kings 21:1-16

1Some time later there was an incident
involving a vineyard belonging to Naboth
the Jezreelite. The vineyard was in Jezreel,
close to the palace of Ahab king of
Samaria. 2Ahab said to Naboth, "Let me
have your vineyard to use for a vegetable
garden, since it is close to my palace. In
exchange I will give you a better vineyard
or, if you prefer, I will pay you whatever it
is worth."
3But Naboth replied, "The LORD forbid
that I should give you the inheritance of
my fathers."
4So Ahab went home, sullen and angry
because Naboth the Jezreelite had said, "I
will not give you the inheritance of my
fathers." He lay on his bed sulking and
refused to eat.
5His wife Jezebel came in and asked
him, "Why are you so sullen? Why won't
you eat?"
6He answered her, "Because I said to
Naboth the Jezreelite, 'Sell me your vineyard;
or if you prefer, I will give you
another vineyard in its place.' But he said,
'I will not give you my vineyard.'"
7Jezebel his wife said, "Is this how you
act as king over Israel? Get up and eat!
Cheer up. I'll get you the vineyard of
Naboth the Jezreelite."
8So she wrote letters in Ahab's name,
placed his seal on them, and sent them to
the elders and nobles who lived in
Naboth's city with him. 9In those letters
she wrote:

> "Proclaim a day of fasting and
> seat Naboth in a prominent place
> among the people. 10But seat two
> scoundrels opposite him and have
> them testify that he has cursed both
> God and the king. Then take him
> out and stone him to death."

11So the elders and nobles who lived in
Naboth's city did as Jezebel directed in the
letters she had written to them. 12They
proclaimed a fast and seated Naboth in a
prominent place among the people.
13Then two scoundrels came and sat opposite him and brought charges against
Naboth before the people, saying,
"Naboth has cursed both God and the
king." So they took him outside the city
and stoned him to death. 14Then they sent
word to Jezebel: "Naboth has been stoned
and is dead."
15As soon as Jezebel heard that Naboth
had been stoned to death, she said to
Ahab, "Get up and take possession of the
vineyard of Naboth the Jezreelite that he
refused to sell you. He is no longer alive,
but dead." 16When Ahab heard that
Naboth was dead, he got up and went
down to take possession of Naboth's vineyard.

Additional reading: 1 Kings 21:17-29

The Good Lie

As a sophomore in high school, I wrote an essay defending Huck Finn's use of deception to save his friend Jim, who was running away from slavery. I would argue a similar position today and would extend it to include the Hebrew midwives, Shiphrah and Puah, who seem to have used deception to defend Israelite babies against the genocidal Pharaoh (Ex. 1:15-22), and also to include Rahab, who deliberately misled the king of Jericho to help two Israelite spies (Josh. 2). I continue to believe that lying to save a life may well be justified. But I have become increasingly aware of how dangerous that position can be.

Once you begin to lie, it's frighteningly easy to continue. I have never had to lie to save a life, but I have lied to spare someone's feelings. As I look back on such "white lies," I see that, though I did not admit it to myself at the time, the person I was "sparing" was often primarily myself. I wanted to avoid embarrassment, conflict, or some other painful encounter, so I lied. But even if I did avoid conflict in the short run, I probably undermined the trust that makes human relationships bearable. If we cannot trust people, we can hardly live with them. Lies deform souls, ruin relationships, corrupt communities, and lead to violence and death.

The Testimony of Scoundrels

The story of Naboth's vineyard illustrates the deadly effect of deception. When two scoundrels testify against Naboth, he can do nothing to defend himself. He loses not only his vineyard but also his life. And Ahab, rather than a relative of Naboth's, is able to take possession of the vineyard because not only Naboth but also his sons (and likely the whole family) have been killed. (See 2 Kings 9:26, which refers to "the blood of Naboth and the blood of his sons." See also Lev. 24:15-16; Josh. 7; 2 Kings 9:21-26.)

Naboth refused to sell his vineyard because he wanted to show loyalty and respect for Israelite legal traditions regarding land ownership. These traditions included the year of Jubilee, which was supposed to occur every fifty years, when families who had sold their property in times of financial struggle were to receive it back. The goal of this policy was to prevent crippling, perpetual poverty; families who needed relief from debt could gain a new start in life.

The social intention of this system is summed up in a key passage from Leviticus: "Consecrate the fiftieth year and proclaim liberty throughout the land to all its inhabitants. It shall be a jubilee for you; each one of you is to return to his family property and each to his own clan" (Lev. 25:10). The theological basis for Jubilee comes out in another verse from the same passage, in which the Lord says, "The land must not be sold permanently, because the land is mine and you are but aliens and my tenants. Throughout the country that you hold as a possession, you must provide for the redemption of the land" (Lev. 25:23). (For additional background on Jubilee, ask your leader for information from lesson 8 in the leader's guide.)

Through the simple but devastating ruse of false testimony, Ahab and Jezebel overturn this entire system of social and economic justice. In addition to lying—or, more technically, *subornation,* which means "deceptively inducing perjury"—they not only murder Naboth and his family; they also rebel against the true owner of the land: the Lord. By stealing from Naboth, they reflect the ideology of Canaanite and Phoenician kings and their gods, fighting against the kingdom of God on earth. And the mechanism for all these sins is false witness against their neighbor.

As Sir Walter Scott puts it in his poem "Marmion": "Oh what a tangled web we weave, when first we practise to deceive."

One Word of Truth

Now that we've noted the relationship between false witness and systemic evil, we can turn with gratitude to the saving alternative of truth telling. Paul captures the life-and-death character of honesty as opposed to lying when he says, "Therefore each of you must put off falsehood and speak truthfully to his neighbor, for we are all members of one body" (Eph. 4:25). Notice how Paul puts truth telling in the service of neighbor love. He teaches the same lesson in his famous phrase "speaking the truth in love" (4:15). We all know how to use factual statements to hurt others and express hatred. But the Scriptures teach us to speak truthfully in a way that "is helpful for building others up according to their needs, that it may benefit those who listen" (4:29). By telling the truth in this way, we obey not only the ninth commandment but also the great summary commandments of love for God and neighbor (Matt. 22:37-40). And, in contrast to Ahab and Jezebel, we defend the kingdom of God on earth.

Alexander Solzhenitsyn illustrates the systemic power of truth telling. A devout Christian who gained fame for resisting communism in the now defunct Soviet Union, Solzhenistyn was once asked how people could resist tyranny without taking up arms. He responded by asserting the power of truth to transform the moral atmosphere of a society. In his acceptance speech for the 1970 Nobel Prize in literature, Solzhenitsyn said, "Let us not forget that violence does not have its own separate existence and is, in fact, incapable of having it; it is invariably interwoven with *the lie*. . . . Once someone has proclaimed violence as his *method,* he must inexorably select the lie as his *principle."* Solzhenitsyn then called for his fellow citizens of the world to resist this evil by refusing complicity in the lie. He summed up his message in an old Russian proverb that says, "One word of truth outweighs the whole world."

How can we resist evil and the kingdom of the evil one? We can speak the truth in love. We can tell the truth for the sake of neighbors and out of loyalty to our King, Jesus Christ.

"That Word Above All Earthly Powers"

As we think about the implications of the ninth commandment for God's mission on earth, perhaps we can do no better than to remember these lines from Martin Luther's great Reformation hymn, "A Mighty Fortress Is Our God":

> The prince of darkness grim,
> we tremble not for him;
> his rage we can endure,
> for lo! his doom in sure;
> one little word shall fell him.

We can witness to the Word made flesh by speaking words of truth. A community that speaks the truth in love and practices what it preaches will attract people to Christ.

Additional Notes

1 Kings 21:1—The narrator calls Ahab the "king of Samaria." Samaria is another name for the northern kingdom of Israel (also sometimes called "Ephraim"—Isa. 7:8-9; 9:9), which split off from Judah (and Benjamin) during the reign of Solomon's son, Rehoboam (1 Kings 12). Perhaps by referring to "Samaria" rather than to "Israel," the narrator alerts us to the un-Israelite way in which Ahab rules over Israel.

21:6—As he tells Jezebel of the answer he received from Naboth, Ahab mentions Naboth's refusal but does not mention Naboth's covenantal basis for this refusal. Naboth views his vineyard as the Lord's land, which has been entrusted to him and his family.

21:7—Jezebel refers to Ahab as "king over Israel." Perhaps her encouragement to Ahab is mixed with scorn for him. She scorns Israelite traditions regarding the king's subservience to covenantal law and the justice and righteousness that flow from the *torah* (see Deut. 16:21-17:20; 1 Sam. 12; 1 Kings 16:29-33; 19:1-2; Ps. 72).

21:10—A more direct translation of the words rendered here as "scoundrels" is "sons of Belial." The *NIV Study Bible* notes, in reference to the same word used in Deut. 13:13, "Later, this word (*Belial* in Hebrew) was used as a name for Satan (2 Cor. 6:15), who is the personification of wickedness and lawlessness."

By calling for two witnesses and prescribing stoning for the offenses, Jezebel uses Israelite law in a deceptive way to defeat Naboth's covenantal obedience.

In the original Hebrew text, the word for "cursed" is actually a word meaning "blessed." Apparently the narrator, wishing to have no association with cursing God, counts on the reader to understand from the context that "cursed" is intended. A similar device is used in Job 2:5, 9 (see "Additional Notes" on Lev. 24:11 in lesson 3).

GENERAL DISCUSSION

1. In addition to the ninth commandment, what other commandments are broken in the story of Naboth's vineyard?

2. Can we really expect political leaders like Ahab to tell the truth?

3. Read 1 Kings 21:17-29. How would you relate these verses to the lesson as a whole?

4. The story of Naboth's vineyard offers a good warning against lying, and other such examples abound. In contrast, how many inspiring examples of truth telling can you think of? Share one or two, explaining briefly why the example is inspiring.

SMALL GROUP SESSION IDEAS

Opening (10-15 minutes)

Pray/Worship—Singing "A Mighty Fortress Is Our God" could serve as a stirring way to begin this session. In your prayer, thank God for bringing you together in the name of Jesus, who is "the way and the truth and the life" (John 14:6), and ask the Holy Spirit to guide you in your discussion, leading you "into all truth" (16:13).

Share—Take time to catch up with one another on how your goalsetting and group projects are going, along with other things in your lives in general.

Focus—During this session try to focus on a question or two like these: *What did Jesus mean when he said, "I am the way and the truth and the life" (John 14:6)?* Or *What does it mean to me that when Jesus said, "For this I came into the world, to testify to the truth" (John 18:37), he was falsely accused and would soon be executed?*

Growing (35-40 minutes)

Read (optional)—You might enjoy reading the story of Naboth's vineyard in a "reader's theater" format. Volunteers can take on the roles of Ahab, Naboth, Jezebel, the two scoundrels, and the narrator.

Discuss—In addition to the General Discussion questions, you may want to reflect on and respond to the following:

- Have you ever overheard someone lying or gossiping about you? Have you ever been caught in a lie or overheard by someone you were gossiping about? Explain how the experience felt.
- Think about times you have lied. Were you more interested in sparing someone else's feelings or your own? Explain.
- How would it (or does it) feel to be imprisoned on the basis of false testimony?
- Can you be honest without being brutal in your words to others? Explain.

Goalsetting (5 minutes)

Consider memorizing Matthew 12:36-37: "I tell you that men will have to give account on the day of judgment for every careless word they have spoken. For by your words you will be acquitted, and by your words you will be condemned."

Or you could simply make yourself aware of this passage and similar warnings and ask God to help you be more judicious in your speech and in your interactions with others.

Closing (10-15 minutes)

Preparing for Prayer—Take a few moments (or longer) to reflect privately on words you regret saying. Mention also any praises or concerns you'd like group members to bring before God in prayer.

Consider reading Q&A 112 of the Heidelberg Catechism:

Q. What is God's will for you in the ninth commandment?

A. God's will is that I
never give false testimony against anyone,
twist no one's words,
not gossip or slander,
nor join in condemning anyone
without a hearing or without a just cause.

Rather, in court and everywhere else,
I should avoid lying and deceit of every kind;
these are devices the devil himself uses,

and they would call down on me God's
intense anger.
I should love the truth,
speak it candidly,
and openly acknowledge it.
And I should do what I can
to guard and advance my neighbor's good
name.

Prayer—Pray again that the Holy Spirit will "guide you into all truth" (John 16:13). Take some time for silent confession before God. Ask for God's guidance in the systems of society and for God's protection and blessing on all who suffer from the effects of false witness.

Why do we break the commandments?

10

DEUTERONOMY 5:21; MATTHEW 15:1-20

From the Heart

In a Nutshell

In the tenth commandment the Lord prohibits coveting—that is, disordered desiring. Positively, the Lord calls us to desire God above all and to order all our other desires accordingly. Matthew 15 helps us to discern what we truly desire as opposed to what we sometimes profess to desire. This passage exposes our hearts and therefore calls us to pray for new (or renewed) hearts filled with the Holy Spirit—so that we can love the Lord by obeying God in all our relationships always.

Deuteronomy 5:21

"You shall not covet your neighbor's wife. You shall not set your desire on your neighbor's house or land, his manservant or maidservant, his ox or donkey, or anything that belongs to your neighbor."

Matthew 15:1-20

1Then some Pharisees and teachers of
the law came to Jesus from Jerusalem and
asked, 2"Why do your disciples break the
tradition of the elders? They don't wash
their hands before they eat!"
3Jesus replied, "And why do you break
the command of God for the sake of your
tradition? 4For God said, 'Honor your
father and mother' and 'Anyone who
curses his father or mother must be put to
death.' 5But you say that if a man says to
his father or mother, 'Whatever help you
might otherwise have received from me is
a gift devoted to God,' 6he is not to 'honor
his father' with it. Thus you nullify the
word of God for the sake of your tradition.
7You hypocrites! Isaiah was right when he
prophesied about you:

8"'These people honor me with
their lips,
but their hearts are far from
me.
9They worship me in vain;
their teachings are but rules
taught by men.'"

10Jesus called the crowd to him and
said, "Listen and understand. 11What goes
into a man's mouth does not make him
'unclean,' but what comes out of his
mouth, that is what makes him 'unclean.'"
12Then the disciples came to him and
asked, "Do you know that the Pharisees
were offended when they heard this?"
13He replied, "Every plant that my
heavenly Father has not planted will be
pulled up by the roots. 14Leave them; they

are blind guides. If a blind man leads a blind man, both will fall into a pit."

15Peter said, "Explain the parable to us."

16"Are you still so dull?" Jesus asked
them. 17"Don't you see that whatever enters the mouth goes into the stomach and then out of the body? 18But the things that come out of the mouth come from the heart, and these make a man 'unclean.' 19For out of the heart come evil thoughts, murder, adultery, sexual immorality, theft, false testimony, slander.
20These are what make a man 'unclean'; but eating with unwashed hands does not make him 'unclean.'"

Additional reading: Matthew 15:21-28

Unbaptized Wallets

A story is told about the "Christianization" of Germanic tribes in the early Middle Ages. As pagans turned from their old gods to the triune God, entire tribes would undergo baptism by passing through the waters of a nearby stream. The warriors in the tribes, however, would keep one arm out of the water, holding their swords above their heads. They refused to baptize their swords because they refused to give up their warlike ways.

Though we can't be sure whether this story is true, it suggests important questions for believers today. What are we tempted to hold outside the water of our baptism? Some would suggest that the most obvious answer would be *our wallets*. When it comes to our checkbooks and credit cards, our mortgages and investment portfolios, we tend to find ways to avoid God's instructions so that we can pursue our own disordered desires. In a word, we covet. *To covet* means "to desire inordinately." And if we may paraphrase the apostle Paul in 1 Timothy 6:10, we may say, "Coveting is a root of all kinds of evil."

Devotion as Sin

In Matthew 15 we meet Jesus upholding the words of God against human traditions. More specifically, Jesus upholds the fifth commandment, "Honor your father and mother," against the hypocrisy practiced by some religious leaders in his day (Matt. 15:4). These leaders would declare some portion of their means and resources as "a gift devoted to God" (15:5). By devoting such a gift to God, they gained prestige for their piety, but they also avoided their obligation to support their parents in the way God called them to. According to Jesus, this form of "devotion" was part of a pattern of hypocrisy in which the people's leaders misused external observances of the law to justify self-serving desires.

Matthew 15 relates not only to the fifth but also to the tenth commandment because the motive for the religious leaders' disobedience is covetousness. The leaders covet money and the prestige they can gain by means of it. These wrongful desires lead them to mistreat their parents while justifying their actions in the name of God. Thus they also are guilty of stealing and of misusing the name of God.

Jesus' diagnosis of coveting leads him to look behind their masks and to see what is truly in their hearts. By speaking in covenantal language about what's "clean" and "unclean" (15:11, 18-20), Jesus teaches that what comes from our hearts reveals the true character of our relationship to God. Neither ritual purity nor impurity matters most of all. Instead, hard-hearted and immoral treatment of others is what makes us "unclean," while obedience to God's commands is what reveals our love for God. (See John 14:21.)

Looking at Matthew 15 in connection with the tenth commandment leads us back to the first two lessons of our study. In lesson 1 we saw that Deuteronomy 6 portrays families united in loving God above all. Here in lesson 10 we find that Matthew 15 portrays families divided as adult children put money in the place of God. This reversal may also remind us of Paul's teaching that greed is idolatry (Eph. 5:5; Col. 3:5). Further, the cloak of piety that the religious leaders use to try to disguise their idolatrous greed may remind us of the golden calf episode (Ex. 32), which we studied in lesson 2. The pretense of worshiping God while really worshiping something else clearly violates both the first and second commandments, not to mention also the fifth—for how could such hypocrites observe Sabbath rest in the Lord when they didn't trust God more than money or more than their own scheming?

In fact, Matthew 15 helps us relate the tenth commandment to all of God's commandments. According to Jesus, the heart disease of coveting leads also to "evil thoughts, murder, adultery, sexual immorality, theft, false testimony, slander" (15:19). Again, as Jesus explains, these things that come from our heart are what make us "unclean," showing that we are violating our covenantal relationship with God.

Why do we break God's commandments? Because we do not love God with "all" our heart (Deut. 6:5; Matt. 22:37). We fall short in our desire for God, so from our hearts comes every form of evil desire and practice. No amount of external religiosity can hide this disobedience from God. Only the blood of Christ can cover our sins, and only the Spirit of Christ can set us free from the power of sin. By exposing our heart disease of coveting, the tenth commandment leads us back to the first commandment, and the first commandment leads us back to

Christ. By his death Jesus saves us from our sins, and by his Spirit he fulfills the just requirement of the law in us (see Rom. 8:1-4). Jesus can give us new (or renewed) hearts, and empowered by this grace we can begin (again) to obey God's commandments.

Devotion as Obedience

Deuteronomy 26 offers a glad alternative to the covetousness and family divisions we see in Matthew 15. Before God's people enter the promised land, the Lord instructs them to respond to grace by making an offering and confessing, "And now I bring the firstfruits of the soil that you, O LORD, have given me" (Deut. 26:10). This combination of giving and worship makes for gladness. The Lord explicitly commands that the Israelites, in solidarity with the needy among them, "shall rejoice in all the good things . . . God has given" them (26:11).

In his book *Deuteronomy and the Death of Moses* Dennis Olson titles his remarks on this passage as follows: "A Ritual of Stewardship as an Antidote to Wrongful Desiring." Olson observes that the faithful practice of responsible financial stewardship helps God's people form habits of faithful giving. And as we do that, says Olson, our covetous desiring "gives way to sharing," which "guards against breaking the tenth commandment." Worshiping, giving, and rejoicing together with our families, we call on God, saying, "Look down from heaven, your holy dwelling place, and bless your people . . . and . . . [all] you have given us" (26:15). In all these ways, we declare that we have chosen not money but God as our Master. We trust that our heavenly Father, who has given us the law for our own good, will also give us everything else we need (see Matt. 6:24-34).

Learning to Love

If we return to Matthew 15 and read a little further, we receive a hint that heartfelt obedience to God's law leads to urgent mission to all peoples. After offending the Pharisees by exposing their covetousness, Jesus, in the next passage in Matthew 15, answers the prayer of a Canaanite woman on behalf of her demon-possessed daughter. At first Jesus refuses to answer her prayer because, he says, "I was sent only to the lost sheep of Israel" (Matt.15:24). But the woman persists in her pleading, and finally Jesus answers, "You have great faith! Your request is granted" (15:28). Jesus' extension of his mission to include this Canaanite woman anticipates his great commission at the end of the gospel of Matthew. There, as risen Lord, he says, "Go and make disciples of all nations . . . teaching them to obey everything I have commanded you" (28:19-20).

As this study has emphasized, we can teach others to obey only as we ourselves learn to obey. We can fulfill Jesus' great commission by obeying the great commandments. God's gift of the *torah* as fulfilled in Jesus Christ equips us to spread God's gospel of salvation to the ends of the earth.

Additional Notes

Matt. 15:1—One important practice for New Testament reading is to see Jesus' disputes with "some Pharisees and teachers of the law" not only as arguments between Jesus and his fellow Jews of long ago but also as living debates that divide churches and Christian hearts today. The sins of hypocrisy and covetousness are often alive and well in our own hearts.

15:2—The "tradition of the elders" includes practices that were intended to promote obedience to the law. Washing hands before eating, for example, was intended not so much for hygiene as for holiness. But when our hearts are far from God, even well-intentioned acts of devotion can lead us farther from God. In *Matthew, a Commentary,* Frederick Dale Bruner states, "Most commentators believe that Jesus did not contest the right or the necessity of Scripture's interpretation, application, and protection—i.e., he did not contest the necessity of tradition—but that Jesus did contest tradition's enjoying *equal* authority with written Scripture."

15:10—Jesus' reference to what makes someone "unclean" reveals his interpretation of the holiness laws that are so important to the book of Leviticus. (See lesson 3 for more on the theme of holiness.) In Leviticus, laws about cleanness and uncleanness as ways to express holiness served not only to guide Israel's relationship to the Lord but also to set Israel apart from the surrounding nations. Jesus calls us to reinterpret holiness in a way that includes having fellowship with all kinds of people. In Mark's version of this story we read additionally that "Jesus declared all foods 'clean'" (Mark 7:19). In doing that, Jesus pointed to the kind of table fellowship with Gentiles that the Holy Spirit taught Peter in Acts 10-11. Based on Jesus' fulfillment of the law, such fellowship is essential to God's mission to all peoples, as Paul argues vigorously in Galatians 2.

15:18—Jesus' reference to "the heart" echoes the great commandment as recorded in Deuteronomy 6 and Matthew 22.

As we noted in lesson 1, the heart is the seat not only of the emotions but also of the intellect and will. With our whole inner selves we either put God first or we desire something alongside or other than God. With these things in mind we can see that the first and tenth commandments form bookends to the Decalogue.

GENERAL DISCUSSION

1. What makes Matthew 15 useful for illustrating the tenth commandment? What other commandments does this passage deal with?

2. Do you agree with Paul that "the love of money is a root of all kinds of evil" (1 Tim. 6:10)? Explain in the context of our consumerist culture today.

3. How does Jesus' use of the words "clean" and "unclean" (Matt. 15:11, 18-20) relate to the major theme of covenant in our study of the Decalogue?

4. How does studying the Ten Commandments relate to the gospel proclamation of salvation by grace through faith in Christ?

SMALL GROUP SESSION IDEAS

Opening (10-15 minutes)

Pray/Worship—Both the opening and closing prayers for this session should be full of gratitude and grace. The Decalogue convicts us, and the tenth commandment is perhaps the most convicting commandment of all. And yet God gives us these

Ten Words not ultimately to convict us and certainly not to condemn us. God gives us the *torah* as a gift of grace for the best possible life and covenant relationship we can have.

The hymn "And Can It Be" would add a rousing worship element as you begin this session.

Share—Take some time to catch up with one another on your goals, group projects, and life situations in general. You may also want to reflect on the question *What permanent effect do you think this study of the Ten Commandments will have on you?*

Focus—Throughout this session try to reflect on the question *Have I prayed for the Holy Spirit to renew and fill me so that I can obey God gladly?*

Growing (35-40 minutes)

Read (optional)—Once again you could consider a "reader's theater" format, or each person could read a verse of the passage in Matthew 15.

Discuss—In addition to the General Discussion questions, consider responding to the following:

- Is *tradition* a good word or a bad word for me? Explain. How can traditions serve the Word of God? How can they detract from the Word of God?
- Are one or another of the commandments especially difficult for me? Are there any I try to avoid facing? Explain.
- What does "heart" mean in the Bible? (See lesson 1.) Do my lips reflect my heart?
- How can I try to do the right thing, even when I don't feel like it—and yet avoid hypocrisy?
- If I confess to Jesus, will he ever send me away? Do I see the heavenly Father running to meet me? (See Luke 15.) Do I ask daily for the Holy Spirit? Share your thoughts with the rest of the group, or simply reflect on these things privately.

Goalsetting (5 minutes)

If you still haven't learned the Ten Commandments by heart, you may want to make it a goal to memorize them now. As you recite the list, think meditatively about each command, asking the Spirit of God to guide you in living joyfully by each one.

You may also want to specify a plan for your own ongoing discipleship and pray for the opportunity to disciple someone else.

Closing (10-15 minutes)

Preparing for Prayer—As you prepare for your closing prayer, mention concerns and praises, including items related to your study of the Ten Commandments.

You may also want to read together a section of Psalm 119. Or read Exodus 34:6-7 as a reminder of the God who has given us the *torah.* You may also want to include an appropriate passage from Jesus' farewell address in John 13-17, such as 13:34-35: "I give you a new commandment, that you love one another. Just as I have loved you, you also should love one another. By this everyone will know that you are my disciples, if you have love for one another" (NRSV).

Prayer—Once again, pray with gratitude, expressing your trust in God the Father's eagerness to give us grace, to fill us with the Holy Spirit, to unite us in Christ, and to teach us the best way to live. Everyone may join in with prayer concerns and praises in the format of a "popcorn" prayer, if you like. Then you could close by saying the Lord's Prayer in unison.

The song "Lord, I Want to Be a Christian" would make a fitting closing hymn, as would "And Can It Be," if you haven't sung it earlier.

EVALUATIONS

Please fill out the evaluation form at the back of this study guide. Your answers and suggestions help us as we develop other studies in the *Word Alive* series. Thank you!

Please mail evaluations to

Word Alive/10 Commandments
Faith Alive Christian Resources
2850 Kalamazoo Ave. SE
Grand Rapids, MI 49560

Bibliography

Brueggemann, Walter. "The Liturgy of Abundance, the Myth of Scarcity." *Christian Century* (Mar. 24-31, 1999).

Bruner, Frederick Dale. *Matthew, a Commentary.* Dallas: Word, 1990.

Buechner, Frederick. *Telling the Truth: The Gospel as Tragedy, Comedy, and Fairy Tale.* San Francisco: Harper & Row, 1977.

Davidman, Joy. *Smoke on the Mountain: An Interpretation of the Ten Commandments.* Philadelphia: Westminster, 1954.

Freedman, David Noel. *The Nine Commandments: Uncovering a Hidden Pattern of Crime and Punishment in the Hebrew Bible.* New York: Doubleday, 2000.

Fretheim, Terence. *Exodus.* Interpretation: A Bible Commentary for Preaching and Teaching. Louisville: John Knox, 1991.

Friedman, Richard Elliot. *Commentary on the Torah.* San Francisco: HarperSanFrancisco, 2001.

Neil, William. *The Difficult Sayings of Jesus.* Grand Rapids, Mich.: Eerdmans, 1975.

Harrelson, Walter. *The Ten Commandments and Human Rights.* Philadelphia: Fortress Press, 1980.

Holwerda, David E. *Jesus and Israel: One Covenant or Two?* Grand Rapids, Mich.: Eerdmans, 1995.

Klooster, Fred. *Our Only Comfort: A Comprehensive Commentary on the Heidelberg Catechism.* Grand Rapids, Mich.: CRC Publications, 2001.

Levine, Baruch. *Leviticus.* The JPS Torah Commentary. Philadelphia: Jewish Publication Society, 1989.

New Interpreter's Bible. Nashville: Abingdon, 1994.

Nielsen, Eduard. *The Ten Commandments in New Perspective: A Traditiohistorical Approach.* Translated by David Bourke. London: S.C.M. Press, 1968.

Olson, Dennis T. *Deuteronomy and the Death of Moses: A Theological Reading.* Minneapolis: Fortress Press, 1994.

Plantinga, Cornelius, Jr. *A Sure Thing.* Second ed. Grand Rapids, Mich.: CRC Publications, 2001.

Smedes, Lewis B. *The Art of Forgiving: When You Need to Forgive and Don't Know How.* Nashville: Moorings, 1996.

______. *Forgive and Forget: Healing the Hurts We Don't Deserve.* San Francisco: Harper & Row, 1984.

______. *Mere Morality: What God Expects from Ordinary People.* Grand Rapids, Mich.: Eerdmans, 1983.

Smith, Betty. *A Tree Grows in Brooklyn: A Novel.* New York: Harper, 1947.

Solzhenitsyn, Alexander. "Beauty Will Save the World." In *The World Treasury of Modern Religious Thought.* Edited by Jaroslav Pelikan. Boston: Little, Brown, 1990.

Stott, John R. W. *The Message of Ephesians: God's New Society.* Leicester, England; Downers Grove, Ill.: InterVarsity, 1986.

Tigay, Jeffrey H. *Deuteronomy.* The JPS Torah Commentary. Philadelphia: Jewish Publication Society, 1996.

Timmer, John. *They Shall Be My People: The Divine Drama from Genesis to Revelation.* Second ed. Grand Rapids, Mich.: CRC Publications, 1997.

Timmerman, John H. *Do We Still Need the Ten Commandments?: A Fresh Look at God's Laws of Love.* Minneapolis: Augsburg, 1997.

Willard, Dallas. *The Divine Conspiracy: Rediscovering Our Hidden Life in God.* San Francisco: HarperSanFrancisco, 1998.

______. *Hearing God: Developing a Conversational Relationship with God.* Downers Grove, Ill.: InterVarsity, 1999.

______. *The Spirit of the Disciplines: Understanding How God Changes Lives.* San Francisco: Harper & Row, 1988.

Yancey, Philip. *Disappointment with God: Three Questions No One Asks Aloud.* Grand Rapids, Mich.: Zondervan, 1988.

______. *The Jesus I Never Knew.* Grand Rapids, Mich.: Zondervan, 1995.

______. *Finding God in Unexpected Places.* Nashville: Moorings, 1995.

Evaluation

Background

Size of group:

- ☐ fewer than 5 persons
- ☐ 5-10
- ☐ 10-15
- ☐ more than 15

Age of participants:

- ☐ 20-30
- ☐ 31-45
- ☐ 46-60
- ☐ 61-75 or above

Length of group sessions:

- ☐ under 60 minutes
- ☐ 60-75 minutes
- ☐ 75-90 minutes
- ☐ 90-120 minutes or more

Please check items that describe you:

- ☐ male
- ☐ female
- ☐ ordained or professional church staff person
- ☐ elder or deacon
- ☐ professional teacher
- ☐ church school or catechism teacher (three or more years' experience)
- ☐ trained small group leader

Study Guide and Group Process

Please check items that describe the material in the study guide:

- ☐ varied
- ☐ monotonous
- ☐ creative
- ☐ dull
- ☐ clear
- ☐ unclear
- ☐ interesting to participants
- ☐ uninteresting to participants
- ☐ too much
- ☐ too little
- ☐ helpful, stimulating
- ☐ not helpful or stimulating
- ☐ overly complex, long
- ☐ appropriate level of difficulty

Please check items that describe the group sessions:

- ☐ lively
- ☐ dull
- ☐ dominated by leader
- ☐ involved most participants
- ☐ relevant to lives of participants
- ☐ irrelevant to lives of participants
- ☐ worthwhile
- ☐ not worthwhile

In general I would rate this material as

☐ excellent
☐ very good
☐ good
☐ fair
☐ poor

Additional comments on any aspect of this Bible study:

Name (optional): ______________________________
Church: ______________________________
____
City/State/Province: ______________________________
____

Please send completed form to

Word Alive / 10 Commandments
Faith Alive Christian Resources
2850 Kalamazoo Ave. SE
Grand Rapids, MI 49560

Thank you!